Growing without Limits

The Modern Guide of Farming with Hydroponics and Aquaponics

Jules Sterling

Contents

INTRODUCTION

Choosing a system is the first step in a successful hydroponic gardening experience. Consider your available space, lighting, budget, and time constraints before purchasing any equipment or settling on a unit to build yourself. Also think about what you want to grow, whether you may want to expand, and recurring costs.

The simplest way to start is with a passive system. These use a wicking material to draw nutrients up to the roots, or the root tips are suspended in a stationary solution with the main portion of the root ball hanging in the air. Passive systems are affordable and easy to build yourself. They are best suited for smaller plants. Active systems are best for larger plants and gardens. An active system uses a pump and timer to flow nutrients around the plant's roots and to provide aeration. It costs more, but is more efficient and requires less attention, since the pump and timer handle everything automatically. Once you've looked at passive vs. active systems, you'll need to choose between media-based and water culture systems.

Media-based systems such as ebb-and flow (flood-and-drain), top-feed (drip), or bottom-feed systems rely on a growing medium to support the plants and hold nutrient solution around their roots. Most operate on timers, alternately wetting the medium to wash out salts and replenish nutrients and then draining so the plants can draw in atmospheric oxygen. Setup is more complex, costs are higher, and media needs to be replaced occasionally. These systems need to be protected from power outages, which can leave vulnerable roots high and dry if the pump stops functioning. On the other hand, these systems are super-efficient, since nutrients are recycled back into the reservoir, and use of timers means they need less attention from you.

Water culture systems usually operate without media. Plants are anchored in a plank that floats on the reservoir, suspending the roots in the nutrient solution. This kind of system is simple and inexpensive to set up and is great for water-loving plants, though special care must be taken if you want to use it with large plants. You can use rockwool cubes or small amounts of gravel to anchor plants like tomatoes and cucumbers that get top heavy when they start to bear fruit. You can also use plastic flaps, foam rings, fiber cups, or plastic collars for plant support, or tie plants to a trellis.

Hydro farm Brings Productive Commercial Technology to Home Hydroponics

Commercial growers have been using efficient hydroponic methods for years. There's no worry about soil-born diseases or pests, and there's no weeding. For professional growers, quicker harvests and higher yields are good reasons to use hydroponics.

At Hydro farm we've adapted these proven techniques to convenient home gardening systems. We have incorporated high performance technology with quality professional-grade materials, and designed a full range of systems for your personal use.

Grow Lights Basics

At Hydro farm we've taken highly effective but cumbersome commercial greenhouse technology and created a broad selection of high intensity lighting systems for both the novice indoor gardener and the seasoned indoor grower. Our high intensity grow lights are easy for home gardeners to use. They come pre-wired and are rated at 120 volts (your normal home current), so they're compatible with any standard home outlet. Just hang them from a simple ceiling hook, plug them in, and start growing.

With Hydro farm's sun-like high intensity lighting, you can turn any room of your home into a virtual greenhouse. Grow any plant, anywhere, anytime you choose! Imagine harvesting fresh tomatoes, picking peppers or growing a rare orchid in your basement – these lights make it possible. A single system can easily provide all the light needed to cover anywhere from a 1' x 2' area up to a 12' x 12' area, depending on what size wattage system meets your growing needs.

Hydro farm's full spectrum fluorescents and lighting systems make it easy to grow the garden you want – whether you're starting seedlings for your outdoor spring garden or growing your favorite plants indoors. Use our lower wattage fluorescents for seedlings, cuttings and low light plants like African violets. Higher wattage fluorescent grow lights provide an excellent starter light for year-round gardening indoors.

Hydro farm High Intensity Lights Are Easy to Use

One of Hydro farm's most important innovations has been to take the effective but cumbersome commercial greenhouse lights and make them easy for home gardeners to use. A Hydro farm High Intensity Grow Light can be hung from a simple ceiling hook and plugged in as easily as a home table lamp.

The systems are completely pre-wired, UL listed (with lens), and ready to plug in. Everything is rated at 120 volts (your normal home current) and plugs into any standard home outlet.

Growing Media

Coconut Coir is an organic grow medium for hydroponic cultivation or amendment to organic soil, excellent air and moisture retention properties, and harbors beneficial micro-organisms.

Organic Soil is rich in beneficial microbiology – it contains its own ecosystem within every bag. Ideal for all stages of plant growth and takes fortification of synthetic and organic nutrition regiments.

Mats improve plant stability and root growth in all tray style hydroponic systems. Root growth is not restricted, but improved, as these mats provide protection from algae and light contamination.

Compressed bricks provide a compact and efficient means for storage and transport of large volumes of coir. Shelf life is indefinite when protected from moisture and sterility is ensured.

Peat pellets, organic plugs, and Rockwool starter cubes are excellent for propagation of healthy cuttings and seedlings. Root systems become well established, increasing the transplant rates of your favorite crops.

Chapter 1: Equipment

By reading this document, the reader agrees that under no circumstances is the author responsible for any losses, direct or indirect, which are incurred as a result of the use of the information contained within this document, including, but not limited to, — errors, omissions, or inaccuracies.

Irrigation

One of the key factors to a hydroponics system is its water supply. Getting the correct nutrient-to-water solution balance is imperative to the growth of the plants and crop production.

Most hydroponic systems work on a recycling principle where the water stored in the reservoir is pumped from the tank to the plant's root system. Once the roots have taken their share of the moisture, what is left over is usually drained back into the tank or cycled off. Most hydroponic systems that do not use the recovery cycle only feed the plants the amount they need which tends to leave little to no waste runoff.

A lot of hydroponics irrigation systems also tap into natural water sources like natural drain runoffs or rainwater tanks. Hydroponic innovative irrigation systems make it possible for arid countries to farm fresh produce.

The irrigation management in hydroponics is a bit more complex than soil-based systems as the water needs to be constantly monitored for its pH and nutrient balance. The irrigation is usually on demand and because of it being a root based system, any sudden changes in the irrigation schedule could do harm to a plant or an entire crop.

Irrigation is generally held in a specific tank that has a balanced amount of nutrients-to-water volume that is required for the nourishment and watering of the plants. The water-nutrient solution is then pumped to the plant's roots by means of a submersible pump held in the reservoir. The water is dispersed by means of some form of hose, sprinkler, or misting system. Or the plant roots are suspended in the water-nutrient solution and oxygenated by an oxygen-stone in the water tank.

There are many different irrigation schemes that work well with hydroponics, aeroponics, and aquaponics. But it is all classified as on-demand irrigation with the plant's water needs determined by its type and environment, such as temperature, vapor pressure, and humidity.

Pots and Trays

Each hydroponic system has its own pots and tray requirements. They can differ quite drastically depending on the hydroponic system type. There are six different types of hydroponic systems.

Pots

The pots are either solid pots with large drainage holes at the bottom, they can be soft and flexible or hard and solid.

Which one you choose depends on what it is going to be used for and is also based on your personal preference.

Pots that are used for systems such as deep water culture, Nutrient Flow Technique, and vertical gardens use netted pots. These are best for systems that require the roots to be free of medium and accessible to the spray or water solution.

Pots are chosen to accommodate both the size of the plant and the hydroponic growing system. They must be able to fit in it comfortably without touching another pot on the grow tray or grow tube.

Deep Water Culture (DWC)

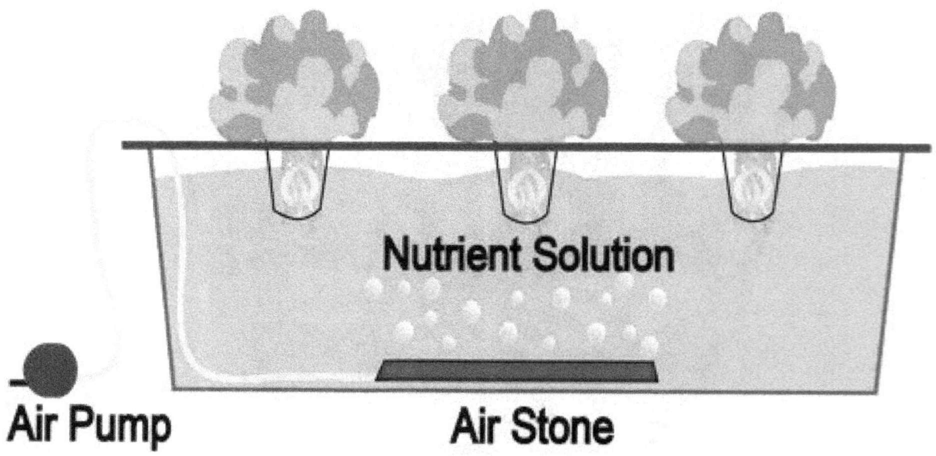

They are usually double the depth of the grow tray and no more than the recommended number of pots for your system should be placed on a grow tray at any one time. This is to ensure that the plants are being fed the correct nutrients and to promote optimum growth and yield.

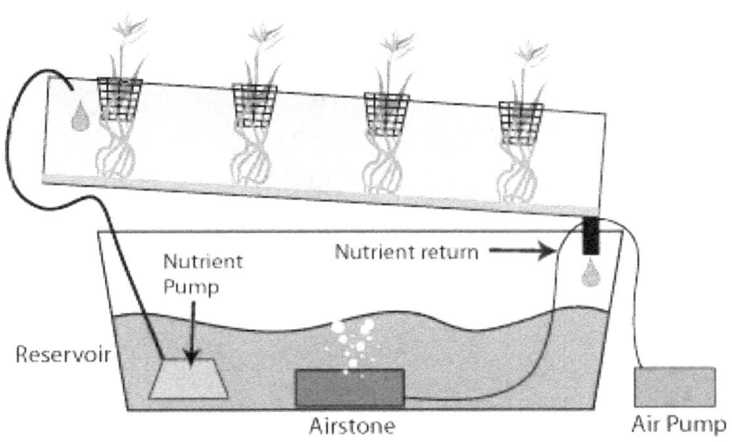

Trays

All hydroponic systems need some form of grow tray, lid, or tube upon which the plant either stands in a pot or netted pot, and is suspended over the water or encased in a grow tray.

The trays come in many different shapes and sizes which cater to a wide variety of different plants as well as the different hydroponic systems. These trays usually have sections where the pots stand, and an inlet and outlet opening for the feeder and drainage pipes.

The tray should be the same size, if not slightly bigger than the reservoir tank and the plant capacity should never be exceeded.

Trays are usually made out of some form of plastic, polystyrene or PVC.

Growing Lights

Hydroponic lighting can be quite costly but is needed in a growing house-type environment. These lights are specifically designed to give the plants the exact lighting they need for the daily maximum required time.

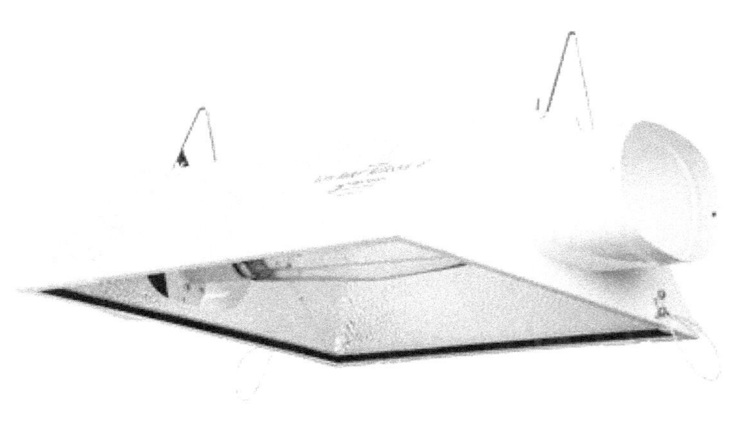

Normal vegetable plants require up to 10 hours of light a day, which can be both indirect and direct sunlight. For indoor hydroponic gardens, a grow light that can mimic something close to this is needed. The lighting system will need to be on for at least twelve hours a day.

To do this a lighting system, an automatic timer is needed; one that is energy efficient is always the best idea here too. The grow lights that have automatic timers can be a bit pricier than the manual grow lights, but they are well worth the investment. Without automatic lights, you could lose an entire crop over one forgetful moment.

Before going out and investing in a grow light, it is important to do some homework first.

The type of light you need will depend on the plants that are being grown, as some plants may need a bit more sunlight than others and so on. For a mixed garden, this will get a little more complicated.

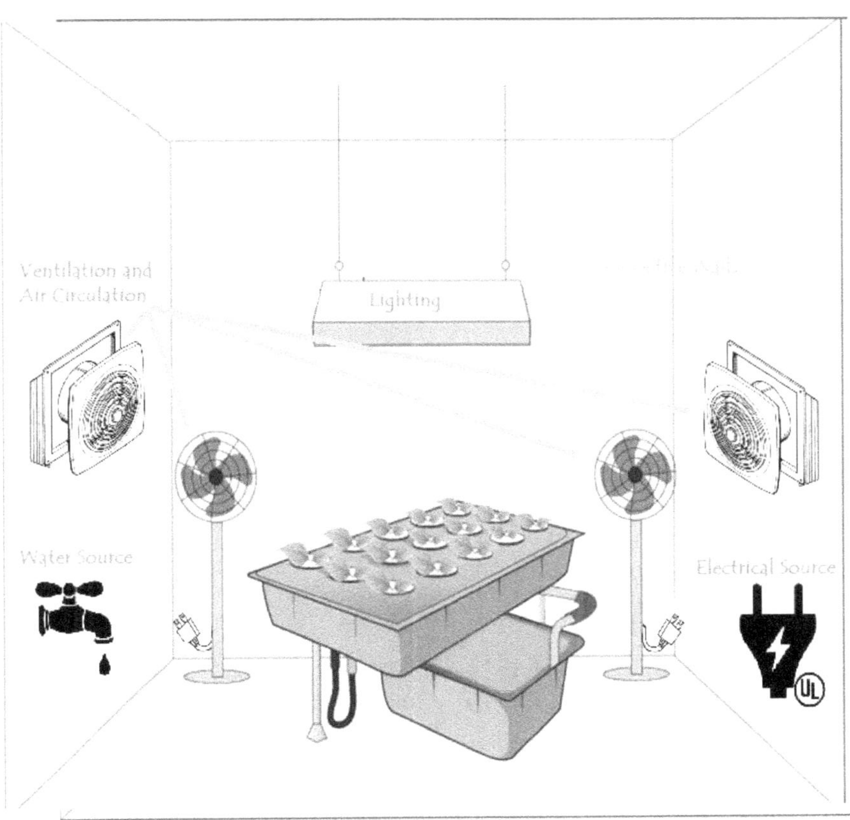

Before investing in a grow light, make a list of the plants that are going to be grown in the hydroponic system. Then check how much recommended daylight they require. From this, a person can start to work out what schedule their plant's lighting system will need. Once a person has a clear cut vision of how and when the light is going to be used, you will have a better chance of choosing one that is right for your growing environment.

All of the components of the grow light must be chosen carefully for your environment. These all have to be taken into account when buying a grow light.

The three main parts of a grow light are the bulb, the timer, and the remote ballast.

The bulb

Actually, this is one of the most important parts as it is what determines the quality and brightness of the light for your grow room environment. Another important factor to take into account with the bulb is how energy efficient it is.

Hydroponics usually need a bulb that is around 400 - 600 Watts. The preference is a HID (High-Intensity Discharge) light which produces a nice pure white light that is the closest to actual sunlight.

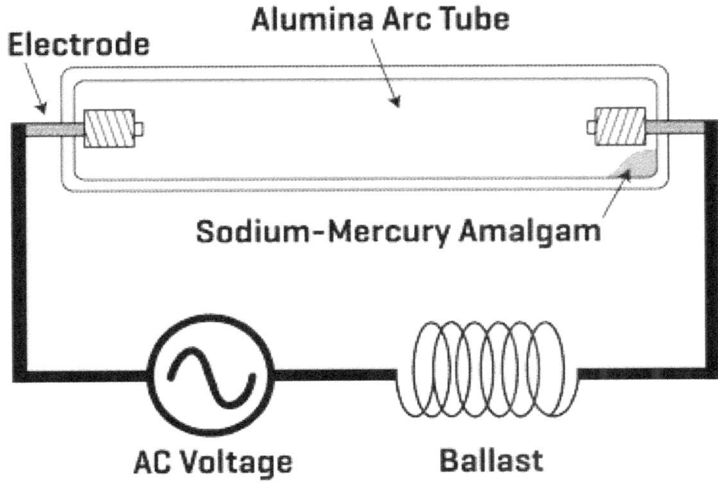

Conversion lamps can easily switch between the two types of bulbs available which are the Metal Halide and High-Precision Sodium bulbs.

The High-Pressure Sodium bulbs are better suited for plants that are starting to flower in the fruit-bearing stage. These bulbs tend to last the longest out of the two types but are also more expensive.

Metal Halide bulbs are the most commonly used and can be used in nearly all hydroponic growing applications. They provide an adequate lighting situation for most crops and will need to be replaced every two years or so as they tend to start to lose their power at around fifteen months or so.

If you can afford it, these two work very well in conjunction with each other.

Timer

Although the lights with timers do seem a bit more expensive, the timer on the lights is not that expensive and can actually cost a lot less than the actual bulb itself.

There are two types of timers, manual and automatic. The manual types use pins to set them. The manual timer tends to be a bit harder and less prone to going wrong or breaking than the automatic ones. They can also be attached to two different lights at the same time. This makes them the more popular choice of the two.

Maxiswitch Solo
MAXIBRIGHT

Automatic timers are prone to breaking, going wrong, and if there is a power outage, they won't work. They may seem a bit more convenient than the good old fashioned manual ones, but they can also be a bit more troublesome as well as expensive.

Remote ballast

This is the box that powers the fancy grow light. They are heavy and very susceptible to moisture so they should be kept above ground level at all times and far away from water or damp conditions.

They are usually sold as a set with the bulb because the ballast has to match the bulb in order to effectively power it. They are usually only used in home system environments.

Substrates and Growing Media

Hydroponics is the growing of plants without soil and using a water-nutrient solution to feed the roots. But some of the system types still need materials to help anchor plant roots, absorb moisture, or provide drainage. This is called a growing medium or substrate. There are different kinds of growing media and the ones you choose depends on the hydroponic growing system being used.

Growing media is divided into different types:

- Organic Growing Medium

  - Coco Coir

  - Peat Moss

  - Pine Bark

- Foam Matrix

  ○ Rockwool

  ○ Oasis cubes

- Grains and Pebbles

  ○ River Sand

  ○ Pebbles

  ○ Lightweight expanded clay aggregate

  ○ Perlite

○ Vermiculite

Equipment for Growing Indoors

The indoor equipment for hydroponics is pretty much the same as it would be for larger hobbyist. Only not on such a large scale.

Many of the hydroponic systems come with ready to assemble kits complete with:

- Growing medium

- Nutrient solution

- Pumps

- Tubing/pipes

- Water Nozzles/sprayers/hose pieces and piping nipples

- Grow Tray(s)

- Reservoir Tank

- Grow Pots

- Set up instructions

The above kit is generally the basis for most of the six hydroponic systems and can be used both indoors and in grow tunnels and greenhouses.

You may need to add a grow light, decent pump, and an oxygen stone but that is about it.

The kit size will depend on the plants that are going to be grown.

All the hydroponic systems can also be done DIY style and most of them are not that hard to make as a DIY project.

The trick is managing the water to nutrient balance, the pH balance, and getting the temperature, humidity, and lighting just right. But these things take practice to master and everyone has to begin somewhere.

Meters

The hydroponic system relies on the quality of the water-to-nutrient solution ration and the pH balance of the solution. Sometimes these values will fluctuate and become a little out of bounds. This is normal especially when the system is a recovery system that recycles the nutrient solution. Each time the solution is used, the plants extract nutrients from it. It also affects the pH balance of the water. The two main levels that need to be constantly tested are the pH and EC levels.

These can both be done quite easily with meters or one meter that can test both.

pH

This is what determines the acidity level of the water solution. It also demonstrates how various plants are reacting to the nutrient mix and how various other organisms are affecting the system.

Each growing environment has its ideal pH range in which it can function normally. Kind of like testing the levels of acidity in a swimming pool to keep it clean and clear. For instance, a good example of an optimum pH range for the growing of leafy greens and herbs would be around 5.5. In order for it to maintain a good balance, the pH level should not move beyond or below .5 each day.

The pH rarely rises in a hydroponic system. It is more common that it will drop. To adjust the pH solution, you may need to simply apply a base solution to the mix.

EC

This is the level of nutrients in the water (also known as the salts in the system) and should be kept within a range of no higher than 2.0 or lower than 1.2.

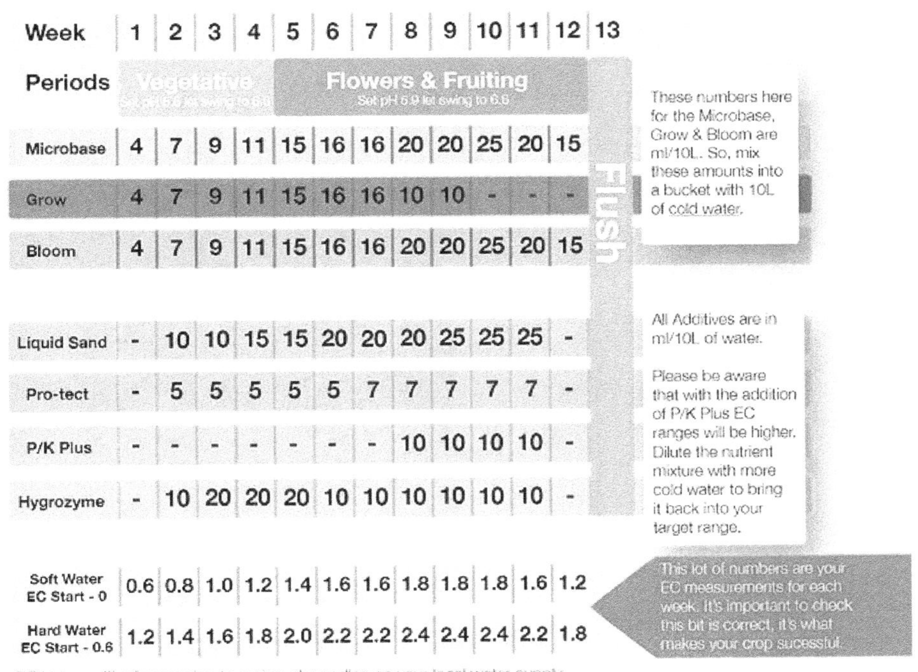

Week	1	2	3	4	5	6	7	8	9	10	11	12	13
Periods	Vegetative				Flowers & Fruiting								Flush
Microbase	4	7	9	11	15	16	16	20	20	25	20	15	
Grow	4	7	9	11	15	16	16	10	10	-	-	-	
Bloom	4	7	9	11	15	16	16	20	20	25	20	15	
Liquid Sand	-	10	10	15	15	20	20	20	25	25	25	-	
Pro-tect	-	5	5	5	5	5	7	7	7	7	7	-	
P/K Plus	-	-	-	-	-	-	-	10	10	10	10	-	
Hygrozyme	-	10	20	20	20	10	10	10	10	10	10	-	
Soft Water EC Start - 0	0.6	0.8	1.0	1.2	1.4	1.6	1.6	1.8	1.8	1.8	1.6	1.2	
Hard Water EC Start - 0.6	1.2	1.4	1.6	1.8	2.0	2.2	2.2	2.4	2.4	2.4	2.2	1.8	

EC Values differ from region to region, depending on your local water supply. So remember to always take a reading of the base water supply before adding any nutrient solutions and add this to the target ranges outlined.

If the EC solution is too high, you simply need to add more freshwater to the reservoir until the level evens out to a more acceptable level. If it drops, you will need to add more nutrients to the mix as per the manufacturer's recommendations.

EC and pH Meters

You can get individual meters to test each one, but it is more economical and easier to get a dual meter. The dual one can quickly help a person determine what needs to be adjusted in order to bring the pH and EC levels back within an acceptable range.

Delivery System

Plants in a hydroponic system rely on three things to help them grow:

- Water

- Nutrients

- Oxygen

There are six different hydroponic systems each offering a different delivery method of these three elements to the plants.

These six systems are:

- Drip Hydroponic Solution: This delivers a steady drip of solution directly to the root of each plant by means of a dedicated nozzle.

- Wick Hydroponic Solution: This system uses an absorbent wick type rope, string, or felt to suck up water to the root system.

- Nutrient Film Technique: In this system, the roots of the plants are constantly in touch with a thin nutrient film that is set to constantly flow over them.

- Ebb & Flow System: As the name describes, in this system the plants are flooded to a watermark with nutrient solution pushed through on a timer then drained until the roots dry out.

- Water Culture System: Here, the plants are floating on top of the reservoir with their roots in constant contact with the nutrient solution.

- Aeroponic System: With this system, the plants are suspended, and their root system is subjected to a light spray of nutrient solution.

Nutrient Film Technique (NFT)

Water flows like a stream in a continuous loop past plant roots.

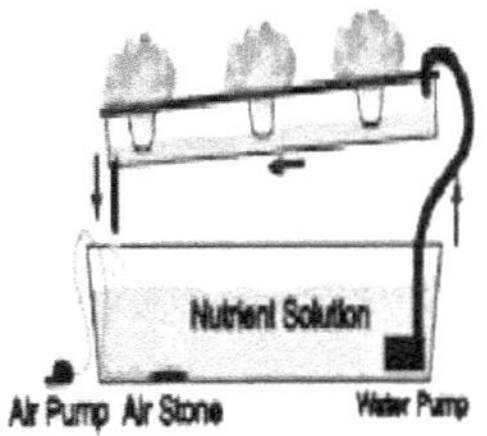

Wick System

Wicks are used to draw water up to the root zone from a reservoir of nutrient solution.

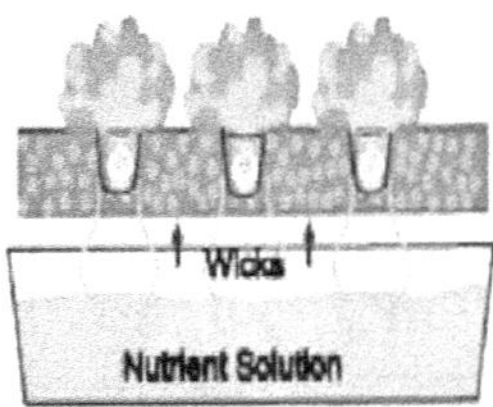

Drip Recovery System

An irrigation line and drip emitters are used to deliver the nutrient solution exactly where plants need it.

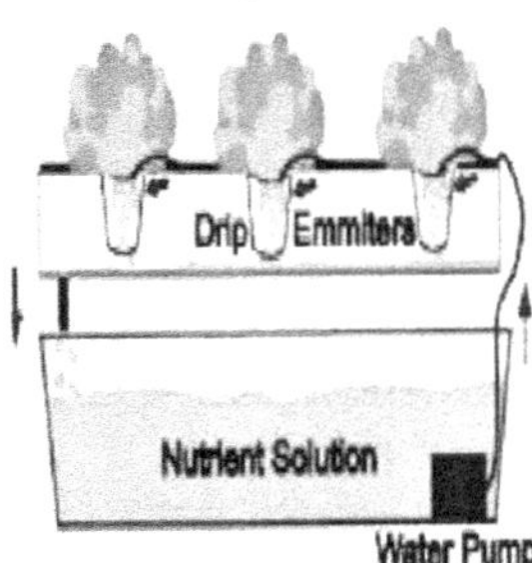

Deep Water Culture (DWC)

Plants float directly on top of the nutrient solution. An air pump and air-stones provide oxygen for the roots.

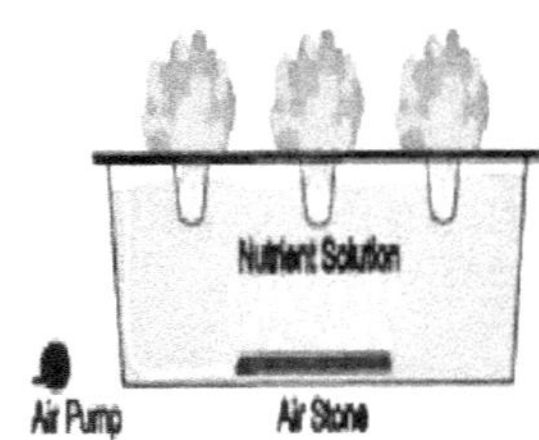

Ebb & Flow

Nutrient solution is pumped into a planting tray filled with gravel or clay pelets. The plant tray fills up with nutrient solution that is then flushed back into the reservoir on a timed cycle.

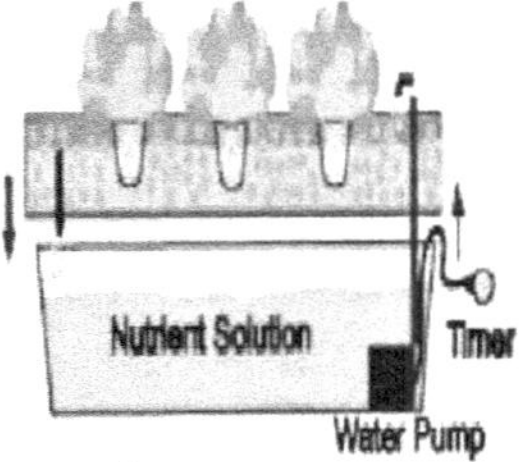

Aeroponics

Plant roots are misted with nutrient solution on a timed schedule.

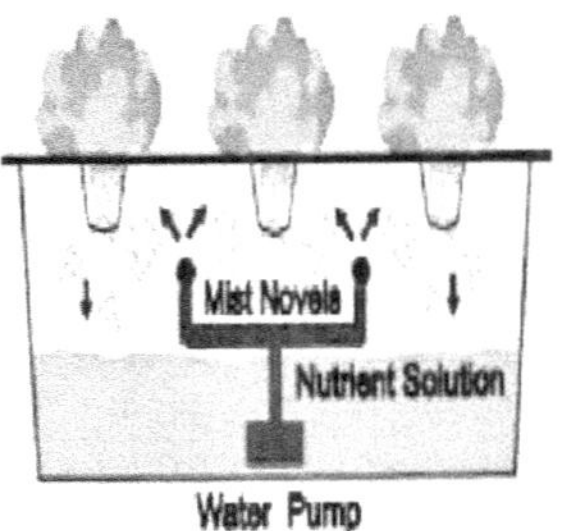

Timer

There are different types of timers that are available for hydroponic systems, from the easy manual pin timers used to control the smaller grow systems to large sophisticated ones that are used by commercial farmers.

Timers give growers more environmental control over their grown rooms. This is a piece of equipment every hydroponic grower will eventually invest in, especially indoor growers.

There are timers that are used to control the lighting and then there are the timers that are used to control room ventilation. Then there are those that are used to control the nutrient solution dispersal intervals. This is perhaps the most important of all the timers as it is the one that determines when and how long the garden gets watered for.

Before you even look at buying a timer you should invest in a power strip that has a really good surge protector on. This is also a necessary piece of equipment that usually gets overlooked until it is too late.

The type of timer will depend on the hydroponic system being used. It will also be dependent on the type of plants being grown and how often they will require nourishment.

The timer will be something that is chosen once the size and type of hydroponic garden have been determined, along with the plants that are to be grown. This does not have to be anything fancy. It can be a standard mechanical timer as long as it can operate in the needed time frame.

Pump

You get air pumps and water pumps with a hydroponic system.

Air Pumps

Usually, a standard air stone attached to a pump is enough to aerate the reservoir tank and feed the plants. When buying an air pump, it should be able to generate at least 500 ccs of air per minute.

The general rule of thumb is that for every 1 gallon of water in the reservoir tank there should be at least 1 watt of power.

Water Pumps

There is no precise way to choose a water pump for a hydroponic system. The only thing to be aware of is that getting one that is a bit too big is better than getting one that may be too small. You can adjust the flow down on one that may be a bit too big, but you cannot increase the flow on one that may be too small.

The pump will be determined by the type of hydroponic system that is being used. The thing to keep in mind when choosing a pump is how high the pump needs to push the water to its designation. Once that is determined a person will have a better idea of how powerful a pump is needed.

Most pumps will need to be water submersible as they will sit in the reservoir and for smaller systems, usually, a standard fish tank pump is adequate.

CHAPTER TWO:
HYDROPONICS VS. SOIL

From an early age, I can remember my parents planting a large vegetable garden. I'd wander through and enjoy a tomato, snap pea, or the raspberries throughout the summer. Naturally, like many growers, this is where I started my foray into gardening- plain ol' soil! However, with our short growing season, I was determined to continue growing my own produce throughout the winter, eventually becoming hooked by hydroponics. Now, with the increase in popularity of hydroponics, the question becomes: hydroponics vs. soil, which is really better?

Before we get into a discussion about which is better, let's quickly define each growing method. Also, let's make sure we are discussing actual soil and not potting mix (here is the difference). Soil consists of silt, clay, and sand, with organic matter, and an extremely diverse microenvironment of microorganisms. This contains all of the necessary nutrients to germinate seeds, and sustain plant growth. On the other hand, hydroponics ditches the soil and uses water containing a customized nutrient solution to induce plant growth. At the same time growing media is used to to support the plant from seed through harvest.

1. Hydroponics saves water

This is by far and away the most important difference when discussing hydroponics vs. soil. Water is at an all time shortage, and the more we can save and put to the best use possible, the better.

Think for a second how the average gardener waters their garden- It is often in 1 of 2 ways. The first (and proper) way is to dump a significant amount of water into their gardens every few days. This ensures good penetration and the development of deep roots. The second and not so proper method is when a gardener stands with their hand sprayer and sprays the soil until it looks sufficiently wet. This group often does this every day, as the water is usually just evaporating. In both cases, only a small portion of the water is actually used by the plant.

Hydroponics allows almost all of the water to be used by the plant for growth. Let's take deep water culture as an example. Plants are grown in net pots or on floating rafts with their roots extending directly into a nutrient solution (water) below. It's nearly completely sealed, leaving no water to be "wasted" through leakage or evaporation. The plants use only what they need, and the rest remains in the container for later use.

In essence, hydroponics allows you to reduce your water usage by around 90% compared to conventional soil based growing.

2. Hydroponics saves space

In a typical soil-based garden, a plants roots need to spread out in the soil to gain access to enough oxygen and water. In a hydroponics system, the plants roots are directly submerged in an oxygenated nutrient solution, allowing them to remain much closer together.

Because your plants are sitting directly in a customized nutrient solution, they are getting the perfect supply of nutrients and air at all times regardless of where the roots grow. When your plants roots are able to stay tighter, you can then save space by planting closer together.

In addition, many hydroponic setups allow you to grow vertically, with several layers of crops above one another. Each layer is typically offset in order for light to penetrate the lower levels. Theoretically you could do the same with soil, but can you imagine how heavy it would be!

3. Hydroponics speeds up growth

Yes, you read that right. Using hydroponics will actually speed up the growth of your plants.

Take lettuce for example- from seed to harvest it will take around 60 days on average to mature in soil. With hydroponics you can cut that time in half, and enjoy your lettuce at roughly the 30-day mark.

So why is it that plants grow so well in a hydroponic system? It is almost entirely due to your control. You are giving the plants everything they need to grow, and the perfect conditions every day. Again, lets compare using lettuce. Out of the 60 days to mature lettuce outdoors, how many of them will actually have a consistent temperature around 21 degrees Celcius (~70 degrees Fahrenheit) and sun for 12+ hours a day. My guess is not very many. However, indoors the plants get these perfect conditions day in and day out. Plus there are no droughts and no nutrient deficiencies.

This all translates into perfect continuous growth from seed through harvest.

4. Hydroponics gives you complete control

Part of the reason your plants are growing so fast is because you have complete control. As the grower, you control the temperature, your control the amount and intensity of the light, and you control the nutrients. You can even control the humidity depending on your setup. This let's you act just like a mad scientist in a lab, tinkering and adjusting these parameters until your grow is just perfect. You become the master of your plant's environment.

5. Far less pests and disease

The beauty of hydroponic gardening is the lower likelihood of encountering pests and disease. Don't be mistaken thinking they don't exist at all, because they do. They are just far less prevalent than in our outdoor gardens.

The biggest threat to our hydroponic systems is usually nutrient deprivation, and thus caused by our own-doing.

6. No weeding!

Many growers love gardening, until it comes time to weeding. When I speak to wannabe gardeners, the largest mental hurdle they have to actually starting is not wanting to weed. I always have great news for this group- start with hydroponics. No weeding necessary!

Does hydroponics change the taste of plants?

This is a complicated comparison. In order to actually understand this question, we must first understand what makes the plant or crop have taste. The nutrients within a leaf, a root, or a fruit create a specific profile, and this profile triggers our sense of taste and smell. The difficult part is our sense of taste and smell are largely subjective from person to person.

So what flavor categories need considering? The common ones are sweet, sour, salty, bitterness, and umami.

Methods to measure flavour

Sweetness can be measured within fruit, leaves, or roots using a refractrometer, and rated by degrees brix (Bx). One degree Brix is 1 gram of sucrose in 100 grams of solution and represents the strength of the solution as percentage by mass.

Another important flavour when examining plants is heat, or spiciness. This is critical when discussing peppers. With peppers we look at the level of capsaicin, which can be determined using HPLC (high performance liquid chromatography) and measured in Scoville heat units (SHU).

After these, measuring sourness or bitterness is very difficult.

The number one reason most people actively avoid eating vegetables is because they are bitter. This is largely due to the phytonutrients present. Phytonutrients are compounds like phenols, isoflavones, flavonoids, terpenes, and glucosinolates. These can boost immune function, help fight cancerous cells, and produce positive health effects overall. However, these often don't appeal to our taste buds.

How does this all relate to taste?

Some plants produce more phytonutrients than others. This not only helps them fight of pests and disease in the garden, but also increases their beneficial health properties for us. The healthier a plant, the more beneficial compounds present, and thus the more flavour.

So if you were a lettuce grower and wanted to sell more lettuce, what is more important to you- a healthier head of lettuce, or a less bitter head of lettuce? Unfortunately, many large food suppliers have started breeding and selecting for plants with less bitterness, and when examined at a cellular level, these plants also tend to have lower levels of phytonutrients. Therefore, they are at a very basic level, "less healthy" for us. Don't get me wrong, you should definitely still be choosing the salad for your side.

The bottom line on taste

The healthier a plant is, the more phytonutrients it will produce, and thus the more flavour it will have. To say wether hydroponics or soil produces a tastier plant is next to impossible. At the end of the day, to produce maximum flavour, a plant needs to be it's healthiest version possible.

There are just as many bacteria and fungi in hydroponics as is soil

Yes, you read that right! Several studies of hydroponic nutrient solutions have found ~10 million (106) colony forming units (CFU) per millilitre (1,2). So let's compare this to the bacterial levels found in soil. Soil structure varies drastically depending on composition, so for this comparison we'll use the best soil we have- compost. The culturable bacterial population in the various stages of compost (mesophilic, thermophilic, and cooling) ranged from 105 to 109 CFU per gram of compost (3,4). Similar to bacteria, Waechter-Kristensen and colleagues found between 10 and 1000 fungal forming units per millilitre of nutrient solution (5).

I know comparing grams of compost to millilitres of nutrient solution is not the most direct comparison, however, it's the best we can do. Regardless, culturable bacteria in hydroponic systems are directly in line with that of compost. Therefore, growing in hydroponic systems is essentially allowing every gardener to grow in pure compost. The fact that not every soil gardener is growing in 100% compost, makes it all even more amazing.

So there you have it!

Not only does hydroponics have some clear advantages over soil based gardening, it also maintains many of the beneficial aspects of growing in soil. Now I'm not about to ditch my wonderful dirt come summer time, it's like therapy digging in the stuff. But the versatility and sustainability of hydroponics is unparalleled, and it will always be a part of my gardening.

Types of Hydroponic Systems

There are six basic types of hydroponic growing systems, each with their own unique benefits that can be adjusted to suit the grower's needs. As such, they can also be combined and customized to fit into different lifestyles.

Overview of the Different Hydroponic Systems

Drip System

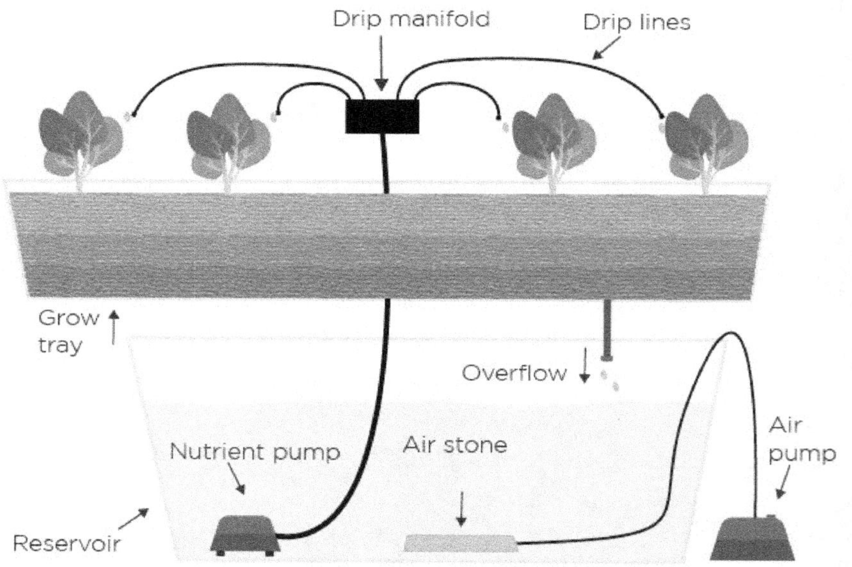

Probably one of the most popular of all the hydroponic systems is the drip system. It is used in commercial applications, on city rooftops, and even in indoor apartment gardens. It is by far the most versatile and efficient system that is also quite easy to maintain.

Benefits of the Drip Hydroponic System

- The drip system is relatively easy to build and maintain.

- The drip system is a good choice for plants with larger root systems.

- The drip system offers the ability to grow plants all year round.

- The drip system has a more versatile watering and feeding schedule.

- The drip system has a very water-efficient irrigation system.

• The drip system is relatively cheap to maintain.

How a Drip Hydroponic System Works

The drip system works by delivering water-based nutrients to the plant's root system by a low-flow method called drip irrigation. It is a very water-efficient system that has little-to-no waste that would normally occur due to evaporation. It provides a controlled and steady slow drip of moisture to the base of the plants instead of showering them from above.

The Working Parts of the Drip Hydroponic System:

Grow Tray

The grow tray is a shallow tray that sits on a shelf or a stand that is around 6 inches above the reservoir. This tray houses the grow pots that contain the plants. The drip manifold is fed through from the reservoir to the grow tray.

Drip Manifold, drip hoses, dripper stick, and drain filter

The drip manifold is usually a specially bought manifold that sits in the grow tray. The manifold has drip emitters that feed the drip tubing. The drip tubing has a dripper stick attached to the end which gets inserted into the growing medium in the pot next to the plant's roots. The dripper stick is what delivers the water-nutrient solution to the roots.

The drain filter is what filters out the overflow and unused solution as it attaches to an outlet pipe that feeds back into the reservoir.

Pots

These are the individual pots that will hold the growing medium and the intended plant. They will stand on the grow tray. They should be of adequate size to house the plants and growing medium. As plants stand in individual pots, it allows for a mixed growing environment where you can grow different types of plants housed in one hydroponic system. In a standard system, the plants would have to have similar watering, pH and nutrient requirements. Commercial growers with special pumps and emitter have a more flexible growing environment.

Growing Medium

The growing medium is an important part of the drip system. It has to be able to provide excellent grounding support for your plant. Most importantly it has to be able to absorb and hold enough water, nutrients, and oxygen to sustain the plants while supplying adequate drainage. The growing medium is inserted into the pots that house the plants in place of potting soil

Growing Mediums that Work Well with the Drip System are:

- Coco coir

- Lightweight expanded clay aggregate

- Perlite-vermiculite mix

- Rock wool

Reservoir

The reservoir, which holds the nutrient-rich water that will feed the plants in the grow tray, is situated directly below the table or the stand that houses the grow tray. It is usually a lot deeper than the grow tray and will house the nutrient pump (with a timer), overflow hoses, and usually an air stone attached to an outside air pump to aerate the water.

The reservoir houses:

- The nutrient pump runs the drip manifold, which protrudes up and through the growing medium. Individual drip lines usually extend from the manifold like a sprinkler system with long sleeve arms. These drip lines each serve an individual plant. Most of them come with a regulator that can be individually adjusted for more feeding control. This makes it easier to grow different types of plants in one grow tray.

- The overflow or return pipes are what drain unused or excess water and nutrients back into the reservoir to be recycled or flushed.

- The air-stone and its air-pump are needed to oxygenate the water by creating little bubbles of oxygen in the water. The pump creates the bubbles and the stone is used to disperse the oxygen into the tank. The size of both the stone and pump needed for the system is dependent on the size of the reservoir tank.

The Two Types of Drip-System

- Non-recovery drip system

In this system, nutrients and water are not recycled as the system has very little to no wasted solution. This is due to the use of sophisticated cycle timers set to a very specific and precise watering schedule. This schedule is defined down to a precise second if need be. It moistens the growing medium around the plants just enough to afford them the nutrients they need. This means there is not a lot of, if any, wasted solution.

As the water nutrient solution is only used once, the system is not as maintenance intensive as the recovery drip systems. Since the solution in the reservoir is not being recycled, the pH and nutrient levels remain constant. Although, it is good practice to regularly check these levels and the tank will have to be refilled when necessary.

It is also advisable that the growing medium for the plants is completely rinsed out with clean fresh water from time to time. This is to stop a nutrient build-up that could jeopardize the system's precise nutrient levels that need to be maintained.

This system is very popular and widely used by commercial growers because of its versatility and ability to control watering down to the second. As it relies on technology and some specialized equipment it can be quite costly, making it more suited to commercial growers.

- Recovery drip system

This is the most efficient system for people who want to have garden hydroponic drip systems. In a recovery system, the water and nutrients are reused over and over again. The water-nutrient solution is slowly dripped onto the base of the plants where it will slowly trickle through the growing medium. This allows the roots to take what they need from the solution. If there is any unused solution leftover, it will trickle back down to the reservoir to be reused.

This system is also known as the recycling system, and while it may be cost-effective saving on nutrients and water, it requires quite a bit of maintenance. Each watering cycle, the plants will take the nutrients they require from the solution which will change both the nutrient level and pH balance of the solution. As such, it needs to be constantly monitored and adjusted when needed.

The reservoir will need periodic emptying out and refreshing of the water-nutrient solution. This is usually the time where growers check their mini pumps, replace air-stones, and any tubing that may require renewing.

Plants to Grow in a Drip System:

The drip system is quite a versatile one and can be designed to grow a number of plant varieties. As their drip can be controlled per plant, they can get as much or little water as the plant requires to thrive. Thus, the drip system caters to both thirstier plants and those that like a drier climate. This system can also be used for larger plants and trees.

These include:

- Most herbs

- Most leafy greens like lettuce, spinach, chard, etc.

- Cabbage and broccoli

- Most commercial vegetables

- Flowers

- Even some fruits like tomatoes, peppers, strawberries, and bananas.

Ebb & Flow

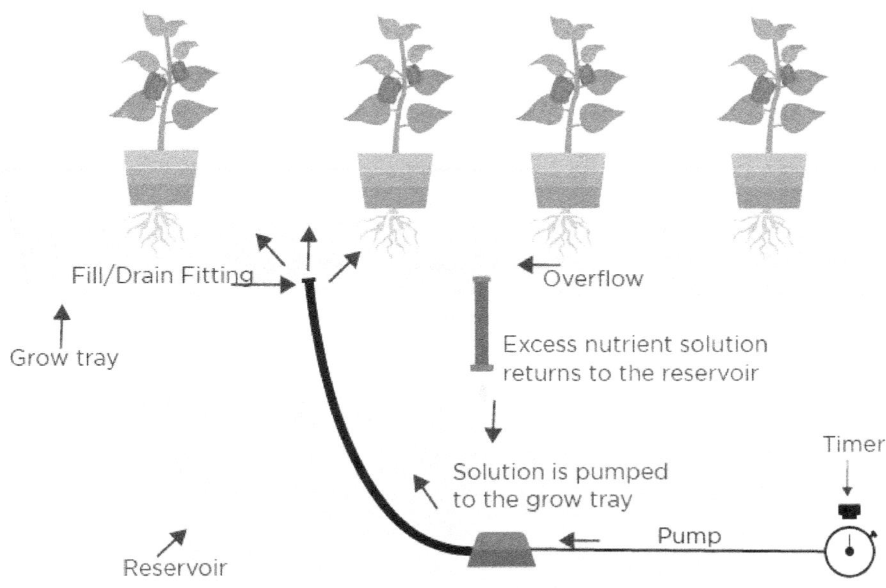

The Ebb and Flow system is probably the system most people associate with hydroponic growing. It is an extremely versatile and cost-effective system to get started but it is not the best for beginners. It is more an intermediate level system.

Benefits of the Ebb & Flow Hydroponic System

- The ebb and flow system is cost-effective to set up and maintain.

- The ebb and flow system does not require expert knowledge to grow healthy plants. Although it will take some training to start.

- The ebb and flow system provides healthy plants all year round if properly set up and maintained.

- The ebb and flow system have a simple watering solution that provides the plants with just enough nutrients.

- The ebb and flow system very water-efficient irrigation system that can reuse water-nutrient solutions.

- The ebb and flow system offers the ability to easily change plants in the planting tray without affecting the rest of the crops.

How the Ebb & Flow Hydroponic System Works

The ebb and flow system may not be the easiest of systems to set up, but it is not the hardest either. Once it is set up it is really easy to maintain and with a bit more experience, a person will find they start to save on various materials. This is especially true if you build the system yourself thus enabling you to scale the project to whatever size you wish.

As the name implies the ebb and flow system means that the plants are periodically flooded with a water-nutrient solution which is then drained away.

It is also called the flood and drain system and consists of two phases:

- Flow (flood)

The system works on a timer that will start the watering cycle. This is done by means of a pump that pushes the water-nutrient solution up into the growing tray. This floods the roots until it reaches the water limit.

The nutrient-based solution is circulated around the tray for a set time.

- Ebb (drain)

Once the roots of the plants have been flooded with the water-based nutrient solution for the set time the timer will go off again. At this point, the pump will stop, and the solution will drain back into the reservoir through the outlet/overflow pipe. This allows for the water-based nutrient solution to be re-used a few times, provided the nutrients and PH levels are kept at the optimum levels.

The Working Parts of the Ebb & Flow Hydroponic System:

Grow Tray or Flood Tray

The grow or flood tray of an ebb and flow system is a large tray that is not too deep. The tray usually sits a couple of inches above the reservoir, on a stand, or on a table. This tray has inlet and outlet openings to accommodate the pump and drainage filter.

Water-Nutrient Inlet/Outlet Pipe, and Drain Filter

The reservoir feeds the flood tray with an inlet pipe that is fed from the submersible pump.

A drain filter is used to drain the water back into the reservoir.

Pots

These are the individual pots that will hold the growing medium and the intended plants. They need to be twice as deep at the flood tray. The base must be large enough to accommodate the growing medium. There must be adequate openings at the bottom for the nutrient solution to flow up through to reach the roots.

Growing Medium

The growing medium for the ebb and flow system has to be strong enough to support the plants. It must not retain too much moisture and has to drain well enough to allow the roots to dry out between flow cycles.

Growing Mediums that Work Well with the Ebb and Flow System are:

- Clay grow stones

- Rinsed gravel

- Sand

- Rock wool

Reservoir

The reservoir is usually twice as deep as the grow or flood tray. It is what holds the water-nutrient solution. This is the solution that gets pumped up into the flood tray and through to the roots of the plants. The reservoir connects through to the flood tray by the fill pipe and draining tubes.

The reservoir houses:

- The submersible nutrient pump that has a timer that gets set to flood the grow tray and turn off to allow the water to drain off.

- The overflow or return pipe is what allows for the ebb of the nutrients back into the reservoir.

- The air-stone and its air-pump are an optional extra. They give the water a bit more oxygenation but as the system is already pumping water up and around it should have adequate oxygenation.

Plants to Grow in Ebb and Flow System:

Plants that do not mind a lot of water and grow quite fast are best suited to the ebb and flow system.

These include:

- Basil

- Beans

- Beets

- Broccoli

- Cabbage

- Chard

* Chives

* Cucumber

* Kale

* Lettuce

* Mint

* Watercress

Nutrient Film Techniques (NFT)

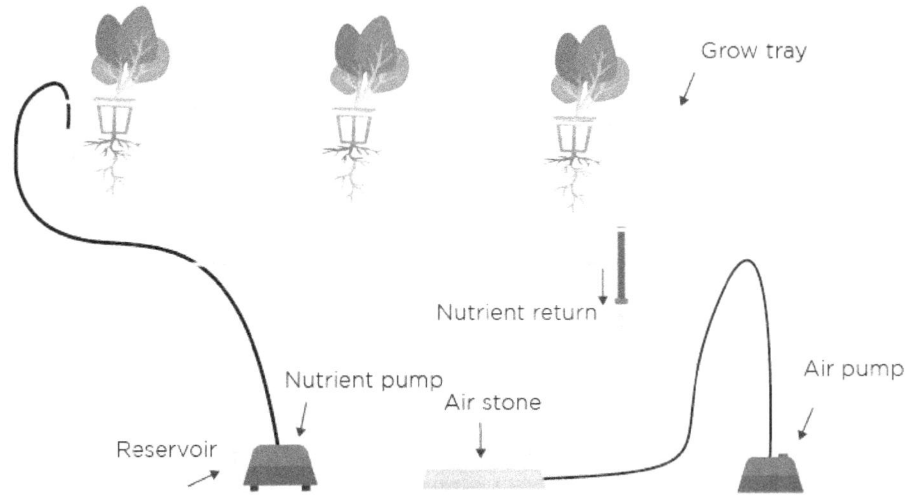

The nutrient film technique (NFT) is a very popular growing technique amongst hydroponic hobbyists and some commercial growers as it is a really versatile system. It has a lot of similarities to the ebb and flow system. But where the ebb and flow floods and then drains, NFT systems run a constant flow of nutrients over the roots of the plant.

Benefits of the Nutrient Film Technique Hydroponic System

- The NFT system a low consumption of nutrients and water.

- The NFT system's constant water flow stops the salt build-up at the roots, it is easy to clean, and has a lower risk of contamination.

- The NFT system needs little to no growing medium.

- The constant flow of water and nutrients creates a thin nutrient film that keeps roots healthy.

- The NFT system is easy to expand because it is a modular system.

- The NFT system is quite easy and not too expensive to main.

How the Nutrient Film Technique Hydroponic System Works

NFT system has a reservoir that contains a water-nutrient solution. This solution is pushed up through a pump into the growing tubes. The growing tubes are usually suspended at an angle so the water flows down towards the outlet pipe that feeds back into the reservoir. The nutrient water solution is reused over again until it is time to change it. A continuous thin film of nutritious solution constantly flows over the roots nourishing them.

Most growers use flat bottom tubing systems that have grooves that run lengthwise along the growing tubes. This helps stop the system from damming up as the water runs beneath the roots.

There should be around a 1:30 ratio which means that there is a one-inch slope for every 30 inches of horizontal tubing length. Keeping the grow tubes flexible means they are easily adjustable as the plant's root systems grow, ensuring that the gully's do not get clogged by the roots.

Shorter tray runs are best to ensure all the plants receive an adequate nutrient solution. Because the water flows down, the plants at the top of the run tend to get most of the nutrient content. A run that is too long may cause the plants at the lower end of the run to become nutrient deficient. That is not to say that long runs cannot be as successful, just that they require a lot more attention to the PH and nutrient balance.

The Working Parts of the Nutrient Film Technique Hydroponic System

Grow Tubes or Channels

NFT systems use channels or grow tubes where most other hydroponic systems use trays or buckets. These tubes make it easier to position them at an angle in order to get the correct water-nutrient solution flow over the plant's roots.

Although some DIY growers use round PVC piping, it can cause uneven watering. A channel with a flat bottom, preferably with shallow, lengthwise grooves at the bottom, is a much better option.

Water-Nutrient Feeding Pipe, and Drain Filter

The reservoir feeds the water-nutrient solution into the grow channel by a pipe attached to a pump. This pipe feeds the water into the channel at the raised end, which makes it flow downwards, constantly feeding the roots as it heads to the outlet drain. The drain filter on the lower end of the channel allows the water to run back into the reservoir to be recycled.

Pots

Most NFT systems put the plants directly into the channel openings, in caps that can gently hold the plant in place. For plants that need more support, seedlings are planted into net pots and they are put into the channel openings. The roots of the plant need to be free to dangle and grow in the channel. This does, however, mean that root maintenance is required in order to stop them from becoming tangled and clogging the system.

Growing Medium

A growing medium is not really required with the NFT system unless it is for seedlings. If a growing medium is to be used it should not be a lot and the roots should be able to protrude through it enough to reach the film.

Growing Mediums that Work Well with the Nutrient Film Technique System are:

- Lightweight expanded clay aggregate

- Diatomite

- Gravel

Reservoir

The reservoir is usually situated beneath the grow channels and the size of it depends on the number of channels it feeds. It is connected to the growing channel(s) by the feeding pipe on the high end and the drainage pipe at the lower end.

The reservoir houses:

- The submersible water pump that runs the water-nutrient solution feeding pipe. This pump runs steadily all the time producing a constant stream of water and as such, is not attached to a timer. This can make the system vulnerable as it is completely reliant on the pump running properly. Blockages or downtime due to a systems failure or power outage could cause problems for the system. The pump should be checked on a regular basis and a backup system installed in case of emergencies.

- The drainage pipe feeds down into the reservoir from the lower end of the channel. This pipe makes sure that water constantly flows through the system and is recycled.

- An air-stone along with a pump to generate oxygen is a good idea and adds much-needed oxygen to the water. The size of the stone depends on the size of the hydroponic system and sometimes two may be needed. The shape of the stone is a purely personal preference although some say different shapes tend to work better than others.

Plants to Grow in a Nutrient Film Technique System:

NFT systems are best suited to the growing of plants that are leafy like lettuce and that have a shorter growth time.

These include:

- Basil

- Broccoli Rabe

- Chard

- Chives

- Dill

- Lettuce

- Spinach

Water Culture

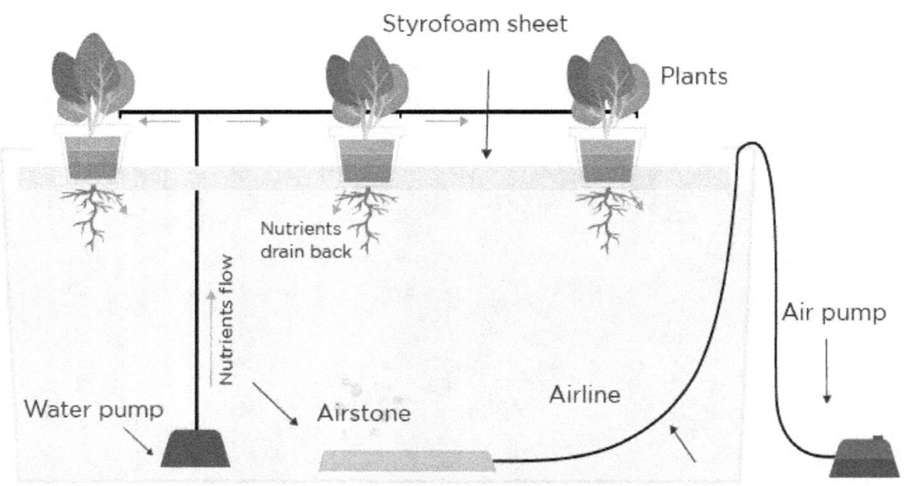

The water culture system is one of the easiest of the six systems to both build, learn, and maintain. It is used with home growers and commercial growers, as the system can be scaled to any size. Plus, there are a lot of innovative ways to design various growing environments.

Benefits of the Water Culture Hydroponic System

• The water culture system is very easy to design and set up.

- The water culture system is not too expensive to get started with.

- The water culture system is quite easy to maintain, and upscaling is not too expensive.

- They are good for just about any size plant.

- They are great for beginners to start with.

- Aerated roots of the system make for faster growth and healthier plants.

How the Water Culture Hydroponic System Works

The water culture or deep water culture is a simple hydroponic solution whereby the plants sit in a bit of growing media in a netted pot. This pot is held in position by a lid that is placed on top of a water-nutrient filled reservoir. The roots of the plant hang freely in the nutrient solution. The water is kept aerated by a pump and air stone.

The Working Parts of the Water Culture Hydroponic System

Reservoir Lid

The reservoir lid is usually made from plastic or polystyrene. It has cup hole openings in it. The size and amount of opening vary upon the needs of the growing environment. The lid must fit comfortably on top of the reservoir and not be too thick or too thin for that matter. The openings on the top of the lid must be just big enough to be able to suspend the plant baskets. The size will vary on the growing requirements.

Pots

The plants will need to be placed into netted pots that allow for their roots to hang freely. The size of the pots will depend on the type of plants being grown.

Growing Medium

The best growing medium for water culture has low-water retention. This is mainly used for starter plants and the top half of the medium needs to stay dry.

Growing Mediums that Work Well with the Water Culture System are:

- Grow rock

- Rock wool

Reservoir

The reservoir is the tank that the grow lid will cover. The tank is filled with water and the required nutrients for the type of plants growing in it. The water should be filled to a level where the roots of the plant sit comfortably in the solution. The water to nutrient ratio depends on the nutrients being used, the size of the growing environment and the plants being grown.

- As the plants are suspended directly into the water solution, a water pump or drainage filter is not required.

- The system does need an air stone and an air stone pump. The pump creates the tiny oxygen bubbles which are dispersed into the tank by the oxygen stone. The size of the stone and pump once again depends on the size of the growing environment.

- The reservoir does require some maintenance and the water-nutrient solution needs to be completely cleaned out and refreshed every other week or so. The water temperature, nutrient and PH balance of the water also needs to be closely monitored in this system.

HYDROPONIC SYSTEM MAINTENANCE

Once a system is designed and built, it is now a self-contained complete hydroponics system that will virtually run itself. There still may be some problems to deal with but if you are vigilant you can catch them early and eliminate most of them.

First and foremost, in my opinion, is to plan now for some means to support your plants as they grow. For a complete hydroponics system without growing medium this is especially important. Even with growing medium it is rarely dense enough to keep your larger plants from falling over when they reach a certain size. I'm talking plants with solid stems growing a couple feet like a green pepper.

And don't be fooled...like I was. A hydroponics plant will grow larger, faster and bear more fruit or vegetables than a similar plant in a dirt garden. I actually tested this when I started growing with hydroponics. It was not a scientific test but the beans grown in the hydroponic system produced faster and had far superior yields when compared to the beans grown in soil.

Now back to the point. To keep a complete hydroponics system complete, meaning running smoothly and efficiently, there are certain periodic maintenance duties to perform to keep your growing system healthy. Let's start with tasks that should be performed daily, or every other day if you want.

Daily Hydroponic System Maintenance Check List

Once a growing system is up-and-running, to successfully grow hydroponic plants, there are only a few tasks required. Check the system daily or every other day and do the following keeping in mind the 5 basic requirements of plants (light, water, nutrients, temperature and oxygen).

Most plants love humidity so mist them continually and they will be happy. Watch the system and make sure it is performing properly. If it floods the plants and drains at a specific time – verify this. Small bits of growing medium can clog the tubing of a system in no time flat and either leave your plants 'high and dry' or continually flooded. This happened to me once.

As your nutrient solution evaporates, add tap water to refill it to where it should be. Do not ever add a touch more of nutrient powder to replace what you think has been used up. This is a really good way to kill your plants.

Keep an eye out for pests and disease as well as nutritional deficiencies.

Take care of any problems as fast as possible or they will grow into large problems faster than you will believe.

Take a look at the plants. Are they wilting and is the growing medium completely dry? Or is it continually soaked? Adjust the amount of nutrient solution accordingly (this is for systems that periodically receive nutrient solution most likely through a timer).

Dead growth saps the energy of a plant and can be a good beginning for a disease or pest problem so keep the dead matter pruned.

Keep track of the temperature if you are in a greenhouse and ventilate if necessary by opening doors, windows and turning on a fan.

In an enclosed area like a greenhouse, let some bugs and breezes get in. This not only helps with pollination but some bugs will actually protect your plants by eating the bad ones.

Learn to identify the good vs. bad bugs. Dragonflies, spiders and 'daddy long legs' are good to have around – they eat the bad bugs so encourage them. I personally love dragonflies – I've seen them dive-bomb horse flies and moose flies and eat them.

Keep a log. What becomes second nature to you now will probably be completely forgotten in a few months so write it down.

I know this seems like a lot of effort but once you get a routine down you may not need more than a few minutes a day to perform these tasks. Keep up the vigilance and you will grow hydroponic plants that are healthy and you will be amply rewarded with a large amount of vegetables and herbs.

Plants to Grow in a Water Culture System:

Deep water culture plants cannot be too top-heavy as they usually need to be supported in some way. They must also be plants that do well in a wet environment, i.e. thirsty plants. Plants like Rosemary that do not like too much water and prefer their environment to be a bit drier will not do well in the water culture environment.

Thirsty plants include:

- Basil

- Broccoli

- Cabbage

- Chard

- Kale

- Lettuce

- Okra

- Sorrel

Aeroponics

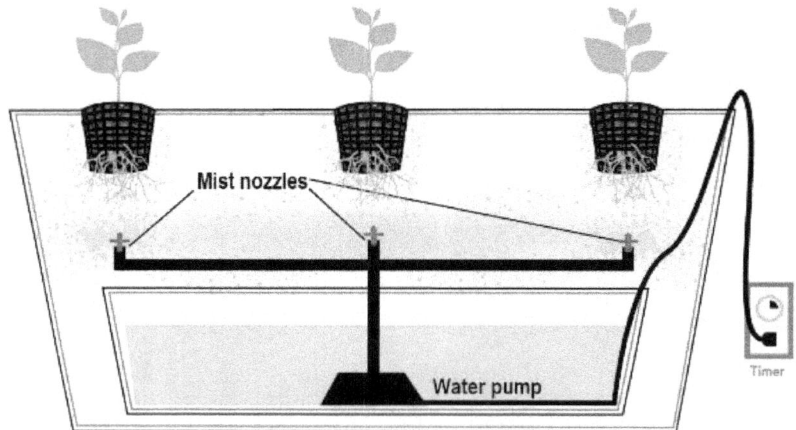

Aeroponics is one of the most efficient of the hydroponic techniques as it uses a misted spray technique to feed nutrients directly to the plant's roots. This is accomplished without the use of a growing medium and affords the roots maximum oxygen exposure.

Benefits of the Aeroponics System

- Aeroponic systems afford the roots a higher oxygen rate which encourages rapid growth and healthier plants.

- They are a good choice for limited space.

- They use less water and nutrient solution.

- They need very little, if any at all, growing media.

- They are a lot easier to harvest than most other hydroponic crops.

- They are relatively easy to maintain.

How the Aeroponics System Works

Out of all hydroponic systems, aeroponics is the most difficult to set up, even though the actual concept is a relatively simple one. The plant is suspended with the roots exposed to the water-nutrient solution in the form of a misting spray. As the roots are suspended, they are able to absorb much more oxygen. Due to the quality of the water-nutrient content and high oxygen exposure, the plants tend to grow a lot faster and are a lot healthier.

The Working Parts of the Aeroponics System

Growing Chamber

This is an enclosed chamber where the plant's roots are hung. It has to be airy enough to let in enough oxygen but at the same time keep pests out. It must also be able to keep in the humidity, water, and nutrients.

Water-Nutrient Misting Piping and Spray Nozzle(s)

The pump will send water through tubing/piping to the misting nozzles for sprinkler heads. These sprinklers spray a delicate stream of the water-nutrient solution onto the plant's roots.

Pots

The aeroponics system does not use pots as the plants are suspended by growing chambers.

Growing Medium

Aeroponic systems only require a growing medium for starter plants such as seedlings and cuttings. Plants that are being transplanted may also require a growing medium. Once the plant starts to mature or liven up and its roots start to form it will no longer require a growing medium. For the plants that do need one it should be a medium that does not absorb or hold onto the water or the plants may become susceptible to stem rot.

Mature plants in an aeroponic system do not require a growing medium.

Growing Mediums that Work Well with the Aeroponics System are:

- Grow rock

- Rock wool

Reservoir

This is a container or small tank that holds the water-nutrient solution. The size and type depend on the growing environment and what type of aeroponics system being used.

There are two types of aeroponic systems:

- Low-pressure system

This is the most common of the two and is used by home growers or hobbyists. It uses a normal pump which operates low-pressure misters that have a light spray and not a "true mist". This system is the least expensive, and easier to set up and maintain than the second option. It delivers larger drops of water than high-pressure systems as well.

- ○ The reservoir for the low-pressure system contains the water-nutrient solution and has a standard submersible pump attached to a cycle timer.

- ○ Tubing attached to the pump runs up to the root zone chamber for the sprinklers.

- High-pressure or True mist

This is a system were an actual mist floats in the air. It is a more effective way of delivering moisture and nutrients to the root system. This is a fine spray with small droplets of water.

- ○ A high-pressure water pump is capable of delivering the necessary misting spray.

○ The tank should be able to hold around 60 psi and the system
    will need specialized misters that can spray only a breath of
    fine moisture.

Plants to Grow in an Aeroponic System:

Aeroponic gardening system is one of the most versatile and can grow a wide variety of plants.

These include:

• Basil

• Chives

• Grapes

• Kale

- Lettuce

- Mint

- Oregano

- Rosemary

- Sage

- Tomatoes

Wick Irrigation

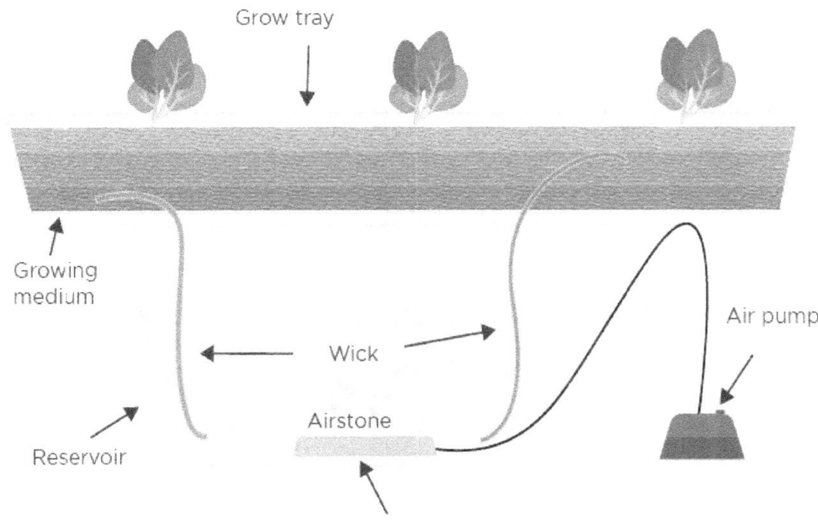

The wick irrigation system is probably the most basic and simplest of all hydroponic systems. That is why they are the best systems to teach beginners and kids that want to learn about hydroponic growing. The wick system is what is known as a passive system as it does not have any pumps (unless if you have an air stone) or drains, etc. This also makes it one of the most dependable of the systems as it is not reliant on any technology or electricity. All it needs is a bit of maintenance and regular check-ups to have you growing plants in no time.

It is also ideal for people who do not have a lot of space for a garden, as the system is very versatile. It is not too expensive to maintain and is extremely easy to get up and running.

Benefits of a Wick Irrigation Hydroponic System

- The wick irrigation system is the easiest of the systems to get started with.

- The materials are easy to source and not too expensive.

- They are very versatile in that they can be a small one with a single plant to a much larger commercial type of system.

- They are ideal for an apartment hydroponic garden.

- They are the best systems for beginners to learn with.

How a Wick Irrigation Hydroponic System Works

The wick irrigation system is best suited for faster-growing plants like lettuce. Although they are easy and cheap, they are not great for growing larger plants that need a lot of water or have finicky watering or nutrient needs. The wick irrigation system works by having a wick or two made from certain absorbent materials. The wicks have one end tucked into the plants growing medium close to the root. The other end of the wick gets suspended in the water-nutrient solution found in the reservoir. The water is fed to the plant through a capillary action that keeps the roots moist in nutrient-rich water solution.

The Working Parts of the Wick Irrigation Hydroponic System

Grow Tray

In a wick irrigation system, the grow tray has the growing medium spread in it with the intended plants planted directly into the medium.

Wick

The wick can be a length of felt, some string, or a rope made of cotton, as long as it allows the nutrient solution to be transported via capillary action to the roots. The number of wicks and length of the wicks depends upon the size of the system.

Pots

Most wick systems do not use pots or netted pots as the plants get planted directly into the growing medium in the growing trays.

Growing Medium

The wick irrigation system requires a medium that can absorb and maintain moisture in order to ensure the plants are suitably fed for optimum health.

Growing Mediums that Work Well with the Wick System are:

- Coco coir

- Perlite-vermiculite mix

- Rock wool

Reservoir

The reservoir needs to be able to efficiently supply the number of plants in the growing arena. It must also be big enough that it does not need to be refilled every other day. The reservoir does have to be cleaned out every now and then to keep the system fresh and working properly.

- The wick system does not need a pump as it is a passive system.

- There is no feeding pipe, so the reservoir is attached to the growing tray by the wicks.

- An air-stone would probably be a good idea in a wick system. As there is no active water flow movement, the stone and its pump help with oxygenating the water to ensure your plants are receiving enough oxygen.

Plants to Grow in a Wick System:

The best plants for a wick system are fast-growing plants that are not very thirsty.

These include:

- Basil

- Lettuce

- Rosemary

Media Beds

Media bed growing is a form of aquaponics that utilizes the symbiotic relationship between fish and plants to water and nourishes soilless crops. The result is fresh healthy food that is grown in an environmentally friendly way.

Benefits of a Media Bed Aquaponic System

- The media bed growing system produces wholesome organic food.

- The media bed growing system cuts down on waste since it's a recycling type system.

- It is a great system for maintaining a fish farm. If not, the fish make a great center point for the hobbyist.

- It provides a cleaner and healthier growing environment with no soil.

- Media bed aquaponics is not that hard to set up.

- Smaller gardens can be set up in apartments or rooftop gardens.

How a Media Bed Aquaponic System Works

Media bed aquaponics works on the same principle of the ebb and flow hydroponic system. Only the plants are being flooded from the water of a fish tank. The water from the fish tank contains all the bio-nutrients the plants need from fish waste products. The plants, in turn, break down the waste in the water cleaning it to be returned to the fish tank.

The Working Parts of the Media Bed Aquaponic System

Media Bed

The aquaponic system uses a media bed in which the entire base is filled with a growing medium. The plants are planted directly into the bed and the system is watered by a pump system that delivers nutritious water from a fish tank. The bed will have the water hose at the one end and a bell siphon at the other end. The bell siphon is what delivers the water back to the fish tank. The water that is drained back has had any waste product broken down in the plant bed. There are times when some growers may introduce specific worms into the gravel of the plant bed to aid in the waste break down.

The size and amount of media beds that can be serviced by a fish tank are dependent upon the size of the fish tank.

Watering Pipe and Outlet Flow Pipe

The watering tube must run from the water pump in the fish tank onto the top or the media bed. The outlet flow pipe will run from the bell siphon back into the fish tank. This has to be set in a way that allows for gravity to drain the water back into the fish tank.

Pots

The plants are planted directly into the grow media in the beds and do not need pots.

Growing Medium

The growing medium needs to be porous and able to maintain enough moisture between watering as well as firmly hold the plant's roots. The growing medium has to completely cover the growing bed.

Growing Mediums that Work Well with the Media Bed Aquaponic System are:

- Pea gravel

- Expanded clay pebbles

- Perlite

- Peat moss

- Coco coir

- River rocks

Fish Tank

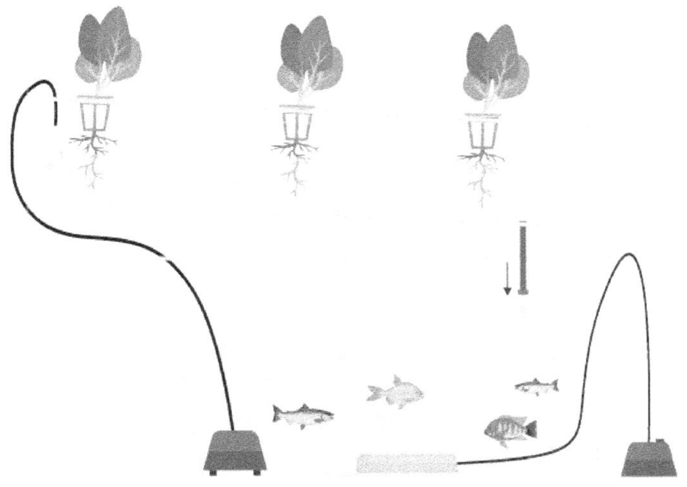

Unlike hydroponics, aquaponics is fed from the nutritious water of a fish tank. The fish tank should be set up with the usual gravel stones, air stone, pump, and of course the fish. It will also need the water pump that feeds the media bed(s) and must be powerful enough to ensure that the water is efficiently reaching and flooding the bed(s).

The drainage system will depend on how the beds are set up, but drainage usually goes through a bell siphon and uses gravity to pull the water back into the fish tank.

The size of the fish tank and the fish that are in the tank are purely a personal choice. A rule of thumb for the size of the tank to media bed ratio is:

- Every 10 gallons of fish tank water can support up to 2 square feet of growing media.

How to Choose a Fish Tank for Aquaponics

When choosing a fish tank for aquaponics you do not necessarily need a big fancy tank. There are many options that are just as good as the top of the line ones. You can even make your own tank from a rainwater tank, etc.

When choosing a fish tank for an aquaponics system, consider these points:

- The tank must be watertight.

- The tank's plumbing fittings must be secure with no leaks or misaligned fittings.

- The tank must not have any toxic material and needs to be sterile.

- The tank must not be made of metal as metal is prone to rust. Corrosion has an effect on the water's ammonia and pH balances.

- The tank must have no plants or other items that can affect the water's pH balance.

- The tank size must be able to comfortably house the type of fish that are going to be used for the aquaponics system. Check how big each species of fish gets before committing to a fish tank.

- Any shape of the tank will do, this is more a personal choice and does not in any way affect the aquaponics system.

- Choose a tank that will fit neatly into the allocated space where the aquaponics system is going to go.

- A pond can be used but you will have to cover it with a pond liner or pond skin. These are usually puncture resistant and help to keep the pond from getting infected by various bacteria, algae and other substances that can be detrimental to an aquaponics system.

Choosing the Best Location for the Aquaponics System

- Only areas, like Florida, that have year round good weather can accommodate an outdoor aquaponics system. You cannot grow vegetables or have fish outside in very cold temperatures.

- If you live in an area that has great summers and cold winters, you will still have to look at housing an aquaponics system in an indoor environment.

- It is possible, to have a system that is outdoors during the warmer months and indoors during the colder ones. There are ways around this; for instance, the system can be moved inside if it is portable or a temporary structure could be set up around the system. However, this is not very cost effective.

- The best solution for an aquaponics system is to have in a greenhouse type environment.

- If you need to have the aquaponics system inside, like in an apartment building, it will have to be positioned where it can benefit from the best lighting. If there is no natural light, artificial lighting will have to be used. If it is possible, combining as much natural light as possible with artificial light is the most beneficial.

- Although it is easier to work with the fish tank does not need to be right on top of or directly next to the grow beds. However, it must be positioned on something that is stable and will not collapse.

- The position of the tank is also dependent on the type of aquaponics system chosen, as deep water culture, media base and nutrient film technique all have different setup requirements.

What Needs to be Included in the Fish Tank:

The most obvious things an aquaponic system needs is some water and fish! But there are few more things that need to go into the tank. These ensure that the system works and that the fish tank produces the nutrients that are required to grow the plants and keep the fish healthy.

- An Air Stone is needed to help with water filtration which is crucial to the success of an aquaponics system. An Air Stone circulates both oxygen and nutrition around the fish tank, which is vital for the water that flows onto the roots. An Air Stone can also ensure that the nutrient solution in the water lasts longer.

- A Pond Filter helps to keep the fish tank cleaner for longer, and stops unwanted bacteria build up. There are two types of pond filters that should be considered:

  o The Biological Filter helps to maintain the water quality in order to keep the fish healthy.

  o The Ultra Violet Clarifier is the filter that keeps away the agents that make the water green.

- The best filter to get is one that does both biological filtration and has an ultraviolet clarifier. A lot of the filters available on the market today do both but it is always prudent to check before buying one.

- A Pond Monitor is a wise investment to make as it continuously monitors the fish tank for leaks, changes in pH and ammonia levels, and water temperature. Some pond filters come with built-in pond monitors and are worth buying. Having a monitor can prevent the sudden unexplained death of the fish in the tank or of potentially losing an entire plant crop.

- A good Water Pump is needed to ensure that the system has enough power to be able to release the water to the crop. It must be watertight, and all the parts must fit snugly together. The pump has to be compatible with aquaponics systems as there should be no toxic components on it. The best pumps have no copper parts that are exposed to the water, are energy efficient, and can work on a timer.

Taking Care of the Fish Tank

- In an aquaponics system, the water is recycled over and over again. The waste matter produced from the fish is used to feed the garden; the garden, in turn, cleans the waste from the water and sends clean water back to the fish tanks. Although the fish are getting cleaned water, the water does start to lose nutrients and still starts to become unhealthy for the fish.

- The pH and ammonia values in the water have to be checked on a regular basis and the fish tank has to be kept clean. There are some tanks snails that can help to clean away bacteria but before putting any such mollusk in the tank, check to ensure they will not affect the rest of the aquaponics system.

- The food the fish are fed can also make a big difference to the water's pH levels and the fish should only be fed food that is recommended for the aquaponics system.

- If the bottom of the tank is lined with gravel, this must be kept clean and changed often. Fish food and some fish excretion can start to build-up on the fine stones in the system.

- Check the fish to make sure they are all healthy as one unhealthy fish can lead to problems for the rest of them. Remove the fish immediately, and clean out the fish tank.

- Remove any dead fish immediately and clean out the fish tank. Replace all the gravel and any air stones.

Fish that Do Well in Aquaponics:

Just like some plants do well in various hydroponic, aeroponic, and aquaponic environments, there are certain fish species that tend to be better suited for the process.

Freshwater fish that like warmer water do better with crops of leafy vegetables such as herbs, lettuce, and cabbage. Tomatoes do better in larger systems that have a lot more fish in the tank, etc.

Some fish species to consider for aquaponics (depending on the size of your growing area and fish tanks):

- Angelfish

- Barramundi

- Blue Gill

- Carp

- Catfish

- Crappie

- Goldfish

- Guppies

- Koi

- Largemouth Bass

- Pacu

Plants to Grow in Media Beds:

Plants that do well with most aquaponic systems:

- Arugula

- Basil

- Chard

- Chives

- Kale

- Lettuce

- Mint

- Watercress

Plants that need a fish tank that has a lot of fish in it:

- Bananas

- Beans

- Beets

- Broccoli

- Cabbage

- Carrots

- Cauliflower

- Cucumbers

- Microgreens

- Onions

- Peppers

- Radish

- Squash

- Sweet Corn

- Tomatoes

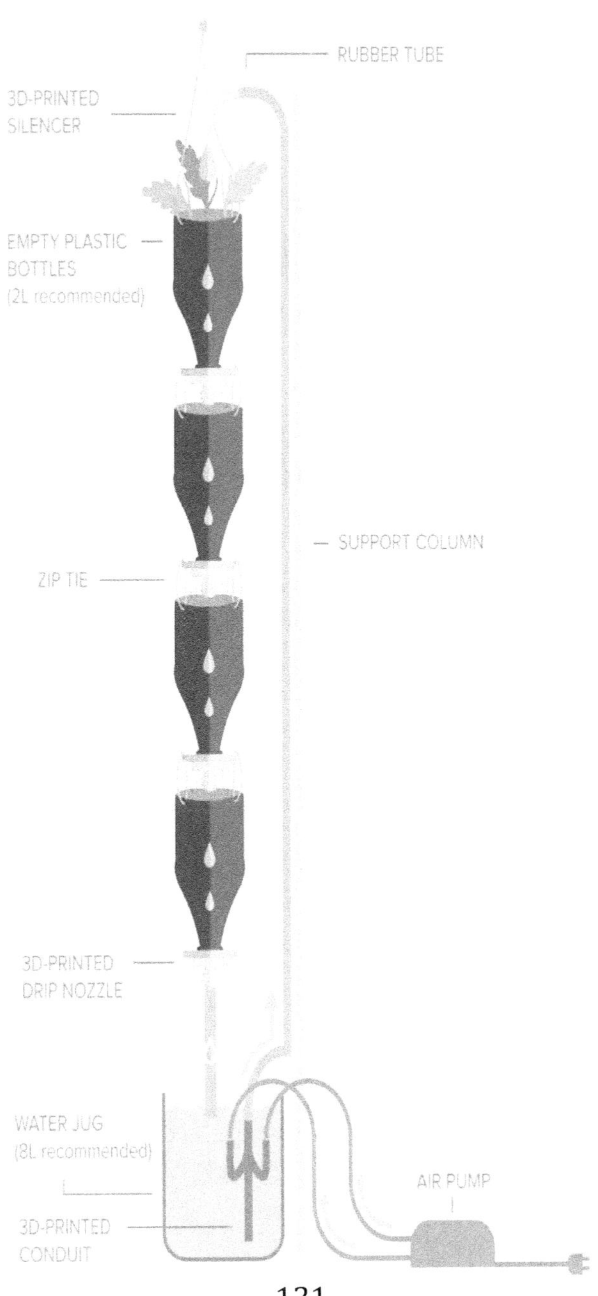

RUBBER TUBE
3D-PRINTED SILENCER
EMPTY PLASTIC BOTTLES
(2L recommended)
SUPPORT COLUMN
ZIP TIE
3D-PRINTED DRIP NOZZLE
WATER JUG
(8L recommended)
3D-PRINTED CONDUIT
AIR PUMP

Vertical Gardens

Humans invented high rise buildings in order to maximize space for both office and home solutions. Instead of spreading out they found the only option was to go up. This is also true for growing space. When you do not have a lot of gardening room to spread your plants out the only other logical way to go is to stack them up.

Places with poor soil and limited space have an option to not only stack up but also to grow those stacked up plants hydroponically. Vertical farming mixed with hydroponics is what brought about the concept of vertical hydroponics. It is also known as vertical gardening, tower hydroponics, or tower garden systems. This allows for stacked level growing where plants are grown at each level. These stacks can be several layers high.

If this concept sounds vaguely familiar to you it is because it is not a new one and has in fact been around since ancient times. One of the many ancient wonders of the world was the Hanging Gardens of Babylon from around 500 BC. It consisted of trees, shrubs, and flowers hanging at different levels in this huge garden.

Benefits of a Vertical Hydroponic Garden

- Soil systems are heavy and weigh down vertical garden. However, there are hydroponic systems that are lightweight and can reduce the garden weight by around 28 to 30 percent.

- They save a lot of space and allow for more plants to be grown which is ideal for the urban grower.

- Hydroponics offers a faster growth rate and you can plant more plants for a greater yield in a smaller space.

- Little to no water and nutrient waste occurs due to the recyclable nature of the system.

- They are aesthetically pleasing, can be soothing and offer other health benefits besides nutrition.

- They are easier to maintain than traditional soil-based gardens.

How a Vertical Hydroponic Garden Works

There are a few hydroponic techniques that could be used for a vertical garden. The two most obvious being the aeroponic systems and the NFT system, although the closed system with a constant flow feeding the roots is probably the better option of the two.

In a vertical tower, a grow tube is used to hold the plants, while a pump pumps the water-nutrient solution out through a single tube that is positioned at the top of the grow tube. The water then runs down through drainage holes positioned over the roots of the plants. This feeds the plant's roots as gravity pulls the water down with the excess draining back into the reservoir.

The Working Parts of the Vertical Hydroponic Garden

Grow Tube

The grow tube is usually a long PVC pipe or similar. The size is dependent on the type of plants being grown and how many layers of plants there are. The grow tube will have an opening up the sides for the net pots.

Inside the grow tube, the net pots must not touch each other, with a blind stop on top of each pot location to stop the nutrients from splashing out. At the top of the tower will be the sprinkler system that the watering hose is connected to.

Watering Tube

The watering tube runs up from the pump in the reservoir and is sprinkled out through a hose bar that is attached to the end of the pipe. The hose bar is usually a bar shape, so the water is pushed out on both sides and the nutrient solution is dispersed evenly through the tower.

Pots

The pots used are flexible net pots that will not break when manipulated into the grow tube opening. The flexible pot is necessary as you will want to be able to easily access the net pots without them breaking.

The pots are positioned so that they do not touch and are well spaced so that each of the plants receives enough water-nutrient solution.

Growing Medium

Grow mediums are a good idea to place in the netted pots as they give the plants extra support as well as providing better aeration and much-needed drainage. The grow mediums should not be too absorbent or hang onto moisture and must allow the root system to breathe.

Growing Medium that Works Well With a Vertical Garden is:

- Lightweight expanded clay

- Growstones

- Rock wool

Reservoir

The reservoir sits at the base of the grow tube tower, it is usually a tub upon which the grow tower fits into. The reservoir contains the water-nutrient solution that feeds the tower.

- The pump must be powerful enough to efficiently pump the water to the top of the tower. It is usually attached to a timer that works for the growing environment.

- The feeding tube or pipe runs from the pump up through the tower to connect to the hose tube for the sprinkler positioned at the top of the tower.

Plants to Grow in a Vertical Garden

Plants that tend to grow quite rapidly are best suited to a vertical garden.

These include:

- Basil

- Broccoli

- Cabbage

- Chard

- Chives

- Cilantro

- Cucumber

- Dill

- Eggplant

- Kale

- Lettuce

- Mint

- Mustard greens

- Peppers

- Spinach

- Strawberries

- Tomatoes

CHAPTER FIVE:
HOW TO BUILD YOUR OWN SYSTEM

How do I get started?

Well, you can buy a kit - but its going to cost you... a lot. Or, you can improvise and create your own kit to suite your needs. My local hydroponic supplier's cheapest multiplane kit is $185, does 8 plants but is not very versatile and is very compact. It uses the ebb and flow method. They also offer a single pot (bucket) bubbler system for $50. We are going to combine these two systems into a more versatile and much cheaper system.

What are my options

There are many different methods. NFT (nutrient film technique - stream a thin layer of nutrient solution over the roots) is common among professional kits - a long with ebb and flow (temporary flood your root system and allow to drain). The most interesting method involves suspending your plants in mid-air and spraying the root system very frequently (aka aeroponics). Drip systems are also common and has its own advantages. There are MANY methods - all of which do not use dirt ;)

What method is used here?

By far the simplest and cheapest is a bubbler system. That is, keep your pots filled with your choice of medium just barely above your nutrient solution level -- then keep the solution well aerated. The popping of the air bubbles will keep your medium moist. Remember that more simple and more cheap does not mean less effective ;)

Cost?

I'm in college - so cost is very important to me. This can be a very cheap project if you collect parts slowly. And luckily, the parts list is not long and they're not rare. I believe I have spent a total of $30 for new materials - however I did buy a few items in bulk and I splurged a little

Why hydroponics?

Hydroponically grown foods not only taste better and are more nutritional, you can change the properties of your food, monitor what goes into your food and pollutes less. You can also grow more in less space. This is especially great for those of us that do not have a backyard to grow in. With the right plant selection, you can also keep pests away. I plan on planting a citronella plant - not only do I like the smell of citronella plants, but their oils keep away mosquitoes and other pests.

Step 1: BOM - Bill of Materials

Parts and supplies

1) 1.Opaque container that can hold water with lid (I am using an old 18 gallon storage bin)

2) 2. Mesh Pots (how many depends on what you're growing and the size of your container - I am using 6 5.25" pots) ($9.90 for 6 heavy duty)

3) 3. Rockwool Growcube (chopped rockwool) (5.95 for three gallons)

4) 4. Growing Solution (I have used Dyna-Grow brand 7-9-5 with excellent results) ($12.95)

5) 5. Aquarium air Pump (nothing special) (already have/not using)

6) 6. Air Stone(s) and air hose ($3)

7) 7. See the start growing step for additional instruction

Recommended but optional

1) Syringe - for making more precise measurements of growing solution ($2.60 for 60mL)

Construction Tools

1) Razor Knife

2) Pencil

3) A compass would be nice

Step 2: Make a Home for Your Pots

Place your pots upside down on the top of your container lid. Now trace around each pot with a pencil making sure that no lines overlap.

Now, if you have a compass, set it to the radius of the BASE of your pot. Eyeball the center of each circle (or measure if you prefer) and trace another circle inside the larger ones.

Next, cut away the SMALL circle and cut perpendicular relief cuts up towards the larger circle (see picture for clarification). The idea is to push the pot down into the hole and the container lid will hold on tight making a better seal.

Step 3: Aeration

My container has breather holes in the handles, so I plan on running my airline through there. You may wish to cut a hole in the top, side or other location. It is not imperative where the hole is as much as it is functional. Keep in mind that you want to keep sunlight out of the container and keep rainwater OUT.

Prep your air stone(s) as per the instructions on the packaging (typically rinsing and a water soak). Please use new stones to avoid intorducing contaminates.

Connect your air stone(s) to your air line and connect to your aquarium pump.

My container has breather holes in the handles, so I plan on running my airline through there. You may wish to cut a hole in the top, side or other location. It is not imperative where the hole is as much as it is functional. Keep in mind that you want to keep sunlight out of the container and keep rainwater OUT.

Prep your air stone(s) as per the instructions on the packaging (typically rinsing and a water soak). Please use new stones to avoid intorducing contaminates.

Connect your air stone(s) to your airline and connect to your aquarium pump.

Step 4: Sterilization

Now, fill your container with water. I am assuming your container is clean and free of debris. Fill to the brim and then ADD 1 TABLESPOON of CHLORINE BLEACH. This is very important as it will kill most intruders you don't want hanging around to cause trouble.

Begin aeration to mix your sterilization solution - put your pots in the container too. After about 20-30 minutes, dump all the water and then allow to air dry completely to get rid of the chlorine.

Once this is done, move on to your initial fill and prepping your medium.

Step 5: Initial Fill

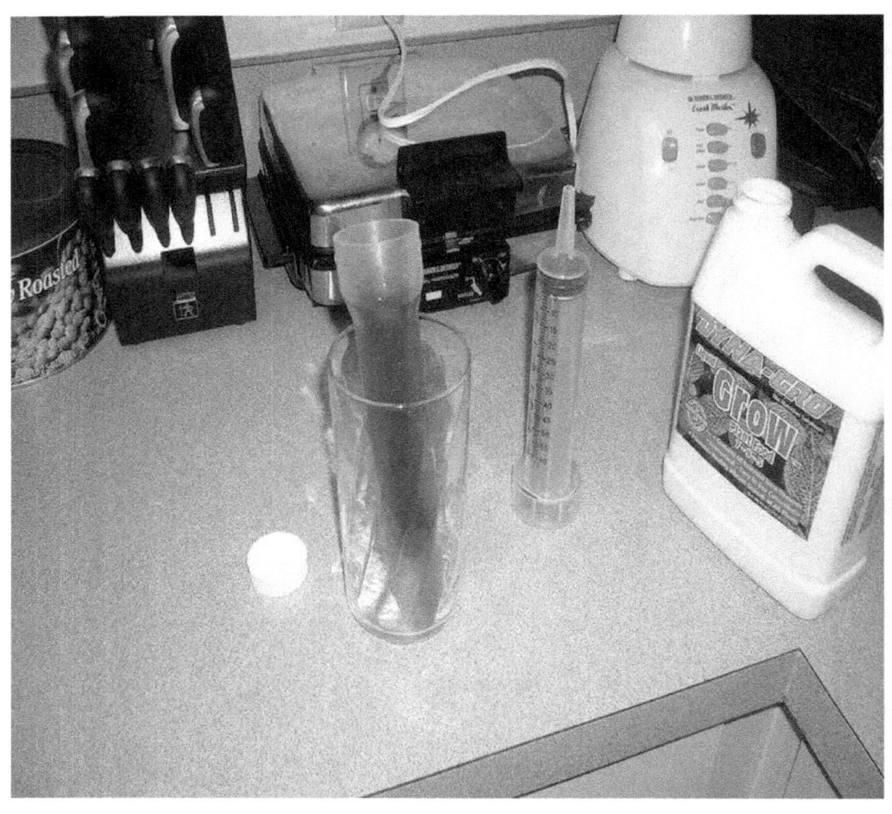

Now, if you've made it this far... you're almost done

Follow the directions on your nutrient solution bottle. My directions call for 2-3 teaspoon per gallon for RECIRCULATING systems and 1 teaspoon/gallon for bag systems. The reason is nutrient toxicity (more on that later). I will treat this as a bag system with a little more.

When filled to the proper level, my container will be holding about 15 gallons of water. So that requires 15 teaspoons of concentrate. Converting to CCs (the graduation on my syringe), that's about 73cc. I will be adding 80cc of concentrate solution.

So, fill your container with water - begin aerating and then add the proper MEASURED amount of nutrient concentration. At this point, your garden should be where you want it as water is pretty heavy, this goes double for larger systems.

Step 6: Introducing Plants and Prepping Medium

I will be buying plants that have already started. I want to grow herbs to start off as I love having them fresh for cooking. So obtain your plants. If you will be starting from seeds, read the next step.

A special note about Rockwool

Rockwool is made from fiberglass... So precaution must be taken. Wear a dust mask while handling and as instructed, soak the medium in water. Water keeps the fibers bound together which further reduces any inhalation risk. The risks involved are no more than handling fiberglass insulation or accessing an attic with fiberglass insulation - just wear a mask ;)

Using a pot, scoop out pot full of growing medium. Rockwool will shrink a little, so add a little more - you do not need this for fired clay. If you have 6 pots, take 6 pot fulls of medium and put it into a large bucket, bowl, etc. Fill this bowl with water and estimate how many gallons you added. Then measure off the appropriate amount of nutrient solution. Completely soak the medium.

While the medium is soaking, wash off all of the dirt from your plants. ALL of it - but take care not to damage the root system. Place a little bit of growing medium in the bottom of a pot, then place the plant in and fill the pot with your medium.

Put the lid on your container, and press the pot into an open hole. Repeat for the rest of your plants.

Step 7: Starting from Seed

If the last step applied to you, you can skip this step -- or read for your information ;)

This requires extra materials - mainly rockwool seed cubes and a method to germinate. But basically, you're going to soak the cubes, drop in a few seeds and then place in your pots with the main media. Be sure that you can see the top of the seed cube. NEVER, put a seed into a dry cube as the dry glass could damage your seed(s)

You're going to need to water by hand to ensure the seed gets the loving it needs. You may want to place a hood over the pot to make the conditions better.

Step 8: Maintenance

Every other week, you need to replace your nutrient solution. Otherwise, the water will become toxic to the plant and it will stunt its growth or cause death. Larger operations don't do this as they have adequate filtering and methods of removing toxins generated by the plants - we don't have this. Besides, the plant is going to soak in those nutrients thus removing it from the water anyway ;)

Monitor your fluid levels in between water changes... If the water gets too low, go ahead and top it off.

When you first start, you want to keep the water level just above the base of the pot. The root system will works its way down into the container (out of the pot) and into the water. When this happens, lower the water level slightly (about an inch below the pots) and make sure to keep aeration going. Aeration prevents the root system from becoming "too wet" and having some of the root system exposed to air helps.

Step 9: Options

So what else can you add on or do?

Well, when you're ready - I recommend adding a water level gauge -
- basically just a clear hose that connects at the bottom of the
container and goes vertical to show the maximum level. This will tell
you when to top off. This will be a future instructable.

Want to grow indoors? You're going to need a grow light -- this adds
a considerable amount of cost but it may be the only option for those
of you in very cold regions.

A simple valve placed at the bottom of the reservoir can make
draining much easier. If yo can drain into a bucket, you can use this
on other plants in your area.

It is a good idea to monitor pH levels and conductivity of your water
solution. I plan on going to my local pool store that does free
chemical testing for pH levels. Once I have some information about
how the pH of the water changes, I won't need to go as frequently.

Step 10: Pests

This is a whole other instructable which will come shortly. But to give
you an idea -- there are plenty of non toxic methods (even non
chemical) of dealing with pests that may arrive.

Step 11: Lighting

I do not own a lighting system... I wish I did, but they can be quite expensive as these are very specialized systems. Regurgitating....

What kinds of lighting are used for growing plants?

Most applications use HID (High Intensity Discharge) lights. All HID systems require both a ballast and a bulb in addition to the socket and reflector. You can also use a T5 High output fluorescent bulb which blends the light spectrum. You can use regular T12 fuorescent bulbs for smaller seedlings and cuttings.

T5?

There are two types of T5 bulbs -- one for blooming and one for growing. Compared to their HID counterparts, they use less heat and all of the spectrum output is used by the plant. The ballast works for both types of bulbs.

HID?

There are three main types of HID: Metal Halide(MH), Mercury Vapor, and High Pressure Sodium (HPS). For growing, only MH and HPS are used.

What do I need for HID?

If you're growing leaf/bushy plants (lettuce, greens, herbs) - you want MH all the time. For plants with a vegitative and bloom phase (i.e. tomato, flowering annuals, fruits) - you want to start with a MH and then swtich to HPS while the plant flowers and starts producing fruit. If all you're doing is supplementing natural light - use HPS.

What if I can only afford one light system?

Here are a few options

1. Use a MH system for growth and then an HPS conversion bulb for flowering.

2. Use HPS for flowering and a MH for growth

3.Buy a standard system and upgrade to an enhanced color corrected bulb. Most go for an HPS system because of the higher lumen output per watt compared to its MH counterpart.

4. Buy a switchable system where the ballast can support either type of bulb

5. Use a T5 system with cool spectrum lamps and warm spectrum for flowering.

What is this conversion bulb?

You can only match a bulb to its ballast (ie MH does not work on an HPS ballast). However, special conversion bulbs will work with the opposite type of ballast.

TOOLS AND WHAT YOU NEED

Hydroponics may sound like a space age way of growing plants. But small scale, simplified hydroponic production may even be used in third world countries to produce enough crops to feed local communities. You can even create a simple hydroponic system at home that will work on your kitchen counter. Hydroponics requires a few tools to successfully grow food.

Flood Chamber

Plants growing hydroponically are either grown in a soil-like substrate that is saturated with nutrient solution, or are supported from above and allowed to float without support in the nutrients. No matter which version of hydroponic growing you prefer, you must have a flood chamber to hold the nutrient solution. Your flood chamber should be opaque so that light will not damage the roots. Rudimentary do-it-yourself hydroponic growers have used fish tanks or mason jars covered by aluminum foil as well as plastic pickle buckets, Styrofoam coolers and plastic storage tubs.

Nutrient Solution

Since hydroponic plants do not grow in a potting soil or another medium that provides nutrients, you must provide all the nutrients that your plants need to thrive. Hydroponic solutions provide the three major macronutrients that are commonly found in fertilizer-- nitrogen, potassium and phosphorous. Hydroponic nutrient solutions also provide the 10 minor nutrients that are not found in fertilizers, but that plants still need to thrive. These nutrients are boron, iron, copper, chloride, molybdenum, manganese and zinc. Beginning hydroponic gardeners can buy pre-mixed solutions with a balance of all nutrients. More experienced hydroponic gardeners may prefer to mix their own nutrient solutions to provide their plants with a customized balance of nutrients.

pH Testing Kit

As plants use a nutrient solution they lower the solution's pH. As the pH of the solution lowers and becomes more acidic, the plants will be less able to remove nutrients from the solution. You can prevent this by changing the solution once it becomes too acidic or by adding alkaline chemicals to the solution. You must periodically test the pH of the solution with a pH testing kit. pH testing strips are available from local pharmacies. Or you can buy a liquid testing kit from a swimming pool supply store.

Lighting

Most hydroponic systems are grown indoors under carefully controlled conditions that include lighting. If you use hydroponics in a greenhouse, your plants may receive some natural light. But even in natural light conditions you may wish to supplement light during short days with artificial lighting. Good artificial lights for hydroponic gardening are a mix of cool white fluorescent bulbs and plant grow lights. This blend provides the right amount of red and blue light waves that your plant will use to grow. You should use one grow light per every two fluorescent lights that your plants grow under. The plants should be placed so that their tops are no more than 12 inches away from the light.

CONSIDERATION TO MAKE WHEN PURCHASING HYDROPONIC TOOLS

Entering the world of hydroponics is very fun and fulfilling, but it can also be somewhat intimidating. There are so many options for purchasing your hydroponics equipment that it can feel overwhelming. While it can be tempting to purchase the first system that looks cheap and easy to use to you, you don't want to wind up with equipment that doesn't match your needs. Here are the most important factors consider when buying your equipment.

Your Available Space – Where exactly will you be growing your plants? A small greenhouse in your backyard? A large closet? Your basement? Before you purchase your equipment, make certain that you calculate the square footage of the space you will be using and figure out exactly how much hydroponics equipment you can put in there. If you are planning on growing rows of plants, try to allow at least one meter of walking space between each row to make it easier to tend to your garden.

Your Plants – You probably already have an idea of what you want to grow hydroponically. Now you need to make sure that you find hydroponics equipment that can help those plants grow their potential. You certainly don't want to purchase small, shallow trays if your plants have larger, thick roots. And you don't want to waste your money on several eighteen-inch buckets if all you want to grow is smaller plants. Talk to your hydroponics retailer about what kind of system, medium, and fertilizer would best accommodate the size and growing rate of your plants. Many manufacturers also have phone numbers that allow you to talk to hydroponics professionals about these kinds of growing issues.

Your Budget – Before you purchase your hydroponics equipment, you should decide upon how much money you are willing to spend, and try to make the absolute best use of that budget. It is important to keep in mind, however, that start up costs aren't the only expense related to hydroponics. You should also try to factor in how much energy your lights will require and how often you may have to replace your equipment. If you plan on keeping your hydroponics system for years, it can save you a lot of money to spend a little extra when you actually buy the equipment.

Your Time – Like most hobby growers, you probably don't want to devote all of your time to growing you plants. This is why you should also consider exactly how labor-intensive individuals systems are. Something like an aeroponics system might seem immediately appealing. But since anything that goes wrong with the timer would result in a very quick drying out of the roots, these kinds of systems can sometimes require more attention than most. Most people simply don't have the luxury of rushing from work to their home to save their plants in the event of a power outage. So look for a system that provides you with a larger margin of error, such as one that accommodates a medium that holds a great deal of air and water well.

Chapter 4: Growing Medium, Nutrients, and Lighting

One of the benefits of hydroponic systems is that there is no soil. In order to compensate for this, the systems need a strong growing medium that stabilizes and supports the plants while also either holding moisture for the plant or draining it away.

In order to feed the plant, because the roots are not in soil, the water needs to have a nutrient solution to properly nourish the plant's roots. Thus, allowing for strong, healthy, fast-growing plants.

Best Growing Mediums for Each System

There are six different hydroponic distribution systems each with their own growing medium needs, although one or two of them do not use a growing medium. Most of the seedlings will start off in one growing medium.

These are some of the most common growing mediums:

- Coco Coir

This organic medium is made from the husks of coconuts. As such it basically has a nearly neutral pH which makes it reusable should it be necessary.

It also retains a good amount of water while supplying an ample amount of oxygen to the root system.

It comes in various different shapes and sizes such as large cubes or small disks for seedlings.

Although it can be used with some hydroponic systems it is not ideal, as it is prone to clogging up systems such as pumps and drains. It is also quite dirty and can add sludge content to a tank.

They are best suited as a growing medium in the following systems:

- Drip Systems

- Ebb & Flow system

- Diatomite

Diatomite is a light, porous growing medium that is made from microscopic algae. This extremely versatile growing medium does not attract insects.

It affords an oxygen-rich environment for the root systems while retaining just the right amount of moisture.

They are best suited as a growing medium in the following systems:

○ Drip Systems

○ Ebb & Flow

○ Nutrient Film Technique

○ Water Culture

● Expanded Clay Pellets

This medium does not keep water soaked up for too long. This makes it excellent for systems that need a fast-absorbing solution that will quickly bring water to the roots then allow it to drain away.

Its pH neutral, insects do not think of it as a great place to lay their eggs, and if thoroughly cleaned and sterilized it can be reused.

It is made from balls of clay or clay pebbles that are round porous balls.

They are best suited as a growing medium in the following systems:

○ Drip Systems

○ Nutrient Film Technique

○ Water Culture

• Glass

The growing medium is one that comes from recycled glass containers, bottles, etc. As a natural substance is porous and offers a highly aerated toxin-free growing medium.

It is used in a foam form and can be used in a wide range of hydroponic applications.

They are best suited as a growing medium in the following systems:

○ Drip Systems

○ Nutrient Film Technique

○ Water Culture

● Gravel

Gravel is a relatively cheap growing medium and can be used in nearly all of the different hydroponic systems. It is also used in aquaponic systems and is a good media bed base.

It can be added to other growing mediums to add a bit more drainage to the mix, which ensures that there is not a lot of salt build-up for the nutrient solution. As salt can become acidic and therefore toxic it is not a bad idea to include a bit of gravel in the growing media if it can be done.

Gravel is not known to retain or absorb moisture but is an excellent support system for plants, ensuring they do not float out of their pots or beds.

They are best suited as a growing medium in the following systems:

- ○ Drip Systems

- ○ Nutrient Film Technique

- ○ Media Beds (Aquaponics)

- • Peat Moss

Peat moss is known to retain water while providing excellent oxygenation to the root system. It is called an "inert organic" growing medium which does well in growing environment that allows for a passive system.

It is very fragile and falls apart easily, so it is not ideal in systems that have a lot of water flow. It is better suited in a wick type environment or with flowers such as orchids.

They are best suited as a growing medium in the following systems:

  ○ Wick system

  ○ Deep water culture

● Perlite

Perlite is a growing medium that is better when mixed with another growing medium such as coco coir or vermiculite. It adds aeration and drainage to another growing medium. It should only make up around a third of the mix.

It can also help to prevent the toxicity of the nutrient solution as it prevents the build-up of nutrients.

There are three different grades of perlite: coarse, medium and fine. It is suited to all systems as it is used in conjunction with other growing mediums to make up a full mix.

• Rockwool

Rockwool is one of the most commonly used growing mediums and is used in nearly all hydroponic systems. It is also known as stone wool as it is made from the heating of silica-based rocks and is spun off into a very thin, wire like material that resembles a ball of more delicate steel wool. This makes a growing medium that is great for oxygenating root systems, retaining just the right water ratio, and as it is pH neutral, insects are not interested in making it their home.

It is very versatile and comes in a few different sizes to accommodate most growing applications. It is really ideal for seedlings as it comes in a small portion and tends to help little plants thrive.

They are best suited as a growing medium in the following systems:

○ Drip Systems

○ Nutrient Film Technique

○ Water Culture

● River Sand

River sand can be used in nearly all applications and is usually mixed with some other medium like gravel, vermiculite, and so on.

It retains just enough water to provide the plants root adequate nutrients and oxygen before allowing the solution to drain away.

The only sand that should ever be used in a hydroponic, aeroponic, or NFT environment is river sand.

They are best suited as a growing medium in the following systems:

○ Aquaponics

○ Drip Systems

○ Nutrient Film Technique

○ Water Culture

● Vermiculite

This growing medium is much the same as perlite only it is mica that is heated to create the medium. Like perlite, it is not a growing medium that is used on its own; rather it is used in conjunction with another growing medium to improve aeration and drainage.

Nutrients For the Hydroponic Garden

Hydroponic garden solutions may all deliver their irrigation systems in a different way, but they all have one major thing in common. Their nutrient-rich solution is water-soluble, as it is delivered directly to the roots with water.

This nutrient-rich solution is full of various macro nutrients that have been specifically designed to deliver the maximum amount of nutrition needed for the growing plants.

Most of these nutrients are delivered from a pre-mix that is in the recommended ratio to the water in the reservoir tank.

This ratio depends on the size of the tank, the delivery system of the solution, and the plants being grown in a hydroponic garden. The granular feeding program is usually provided with the mix in order to help the gardener get the correct nutrient and pH balance ratios for the growing system.

The electrical conductivity, or EC, of the mix is how the concentration of the mix is measured. The EC of the nutrient mix can be measured with an EC meter once the mix has been dissolved in a tank of water.

Plants need the following macronutrients for optimum growth:

- Calcium

- Iron

- Magnesium

- Nitrogen

- Phosphorus

- Potassium

- Sulfur

They will also have to have controlled levels of the following nutrients:

- Boron

- Copper

- Manganese

- Molybdenum

- Zinc

The pH Balance

Not only do the nutrient levels need to properly balance and controlled but for the plants to be able to efficiently absorb these nutrients, the acidity levels in their water solution have to be just right. This balance is called the pH balance and should be between 5.5 and 6.5 as discussed in an earlier chapter.

The pH is the concentration of hydrogen ion levels that can be found in a certain solution like water. It is also found in various nutrient solutions and soil content.

Levels of pH are measured on a scale of 0 - 14. With anything above 7 being acidic and anything below 7 is considered neutral or normal. If the nutrient solution is mixed with the correct solution to water ratio for the Hydroponic system, the pH balance will be normal.

The table below, points out some of the main points of each medium.

Medium	Good Drainage	Water Retention	Oxygen Retention	Good Stability	Can Dry Out
*Rockwool Fiber *Melted Basalt	✓	✓	✓	✓	✓
*River Rock	✓	X	✓	✓	✓
*Pumice	✓	✓	✓	✓	✓
* Clay Pellets *Hydrocorn *Hydroton	✓	X	✓	✓	✓
*Sand	✓	X	X	✓	✓
*Composted	✓	✓	✓	✓	✓

Pine Bark

*Coco Coir	✓	✓	✓	✓	✓
*Coco chips					
*Vermiculite	✗	✓	✗	✓	✗
*Perlite	✓	✗	✓	✓	✗

Lighting

The lighting for a hydroponics system is extremely important. Especially for seedlings. If seedlings do not get enough light, they tend to get long and spindly, with weird-shaped leaves. This is because they try to stretch towards the light.

Even larger plants need a lot of light, usually up to fourteen hours a day, and seedlings need up to sixteen hours of sunlight a day. If you are growing just one or two little boxes of seedlings or a large plant or two, it is easy to pop them onto a sunny window ledge for the day. Although even that is not an ideal situation, because the concentration of the light can also affect the plants.

Just like the nutrient solution has to be the perfect ratio of water to nutrient, and then timed perfectly to water the plants, the lighting has to be done in a similar way. It must be timed to give the plants almost the exact amount of imitated sunlight a day and it must be set at the right intensity so as not to burn the plants or give too little that they are cold.

Balance is crucial for hydroponics system in order to make the system function correctly and produce healthy, nutritious plants. In order to get sunlight to the plants in a hydroponic system, one would have to have a grow light, preferably one that is set to a timer. Having to manually start and then stop the timer may save on buying costs of the timer, but it could also lead to a whole lot of problems.

Pros of manually setting the growing light timer:

- Saves on the cost of buying an automatic timer.

- It allows a person to control the times they switch the lights on and off.

- It can be efficient in energy management.

Cons of manually setting the growing light timer:

- Possibility of human error.

- Possibility of losing entire crops due to human error.

- Very time consuming and the gardener's day has to be timed around being able to switch the timers on and off to ensure maximum growing health.

Granted some of the fanciest timers can be quite expensive but to start out, all a person needs is a mechanical timer with the pins. These are more than adequate for setting up the lighting timers for a few days up to two weeks at a time. Some of them can be shared between two devices.

There are also inexpensive digital ones that may not have all the bells and whistles but still do everything that needs to be done. If you are going to have growing lights, you are going to need a timer.

Pros of a growing light timer:

- No human error

- The timer switches the lights on and off at the exact times the plants need the lights on and off.

- Except for checking to see if the timer is working, the gardener's day does not have to revolve around rushing to ensure they switch the lights on and off at a precise time each day.

- Happy plants that have their needed sunlight time, when and how they need it.

Cons of a growing light timer:

- An initial cost outlay.

- Digital or electrical timers are reliant on electricity.

The Advantages of Using Growing Lights:

- Seeds germinate more rapidly in the correct light.

- Winter germination of seedlings is more successful.

- Seedlings grow up healthier, their growth is not stunted, and in some cases, their growth rate is increased.

- Plants need more daylight hours, some up to fourteen hours a day. This is hard to achieve with natural sunlight and in winter it is impossible. Growing lights make having fourteen hours a day of uninterrupted light possible all year round.

- The correct light in the growing room helps to keep the entire environment healthy, especially if the environmental conditions are all balanced. Such as the correct ventilation for optimum airflow. This promotes good air quality and the correct amount of light to provide both a bit of warmth and light.

The Best Color Growing Lights for Plants

To humans, sunlight is that big yellow ball of light in the sky that makes everything bright yellow or white. But daylight in respect to color is a bit more complex than that. The light we see is what is known as visible light, that is seen through frequencies and wavelengths the human eye can interpret.

What are Spectrums?

Light itself is made up of various spectrums of color that can be interpreted at different wavelengths which is the reason light is described in frequencies or wavelengths. For instance, when you look at a rainbow each color comes back to the human eye at different frequencies. Each color is a different spectrum, and most grow lights only need a dual spectrum light. Dual spectrum means two colors, and for optimum growth those two-color spectrums are red and blue.

Full Spectrum Growing Lights

A full spectrum light is not very energy efficient and can get quite hot as it is usually a fluorescent light that is designed to emulate the midday sun. It does have cool and warm tones, but it is better for a larger growing area with the need for stronger lighting. It could be a bit of overkill for a small-scale growing area.

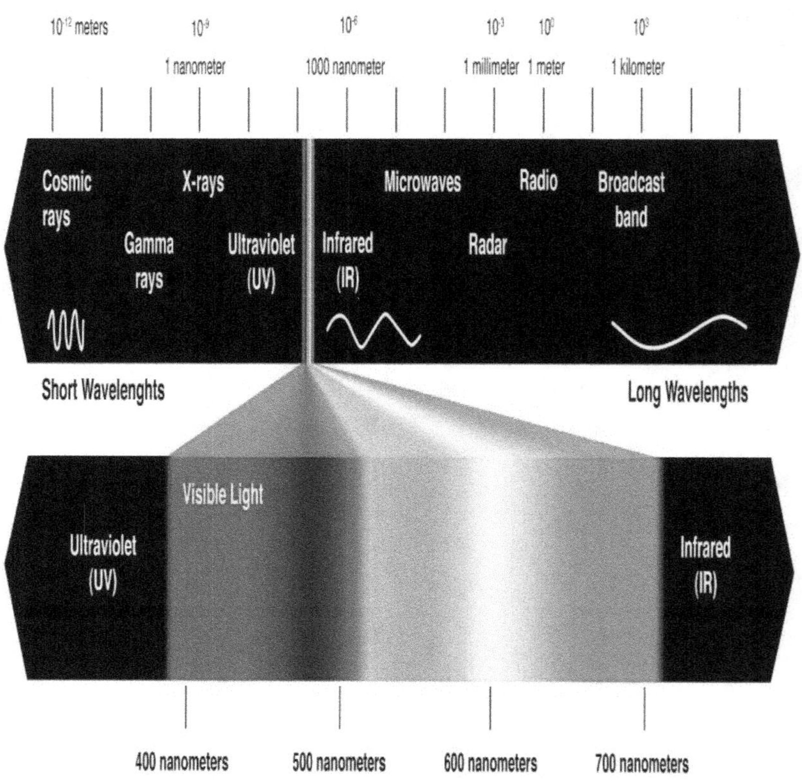

High-Intensity Discharge (HID) Growing Lights

These are the brightest and most used of all the grow lights. They are a light that is powered by a glass tube containing a gas, usually xenon, that can emit up to 800 watts of light. This light is a lot more energy efficient than fluorescent lights and is more than adequate for a healthy indoor garden.

There are two kinds of HID lights:

- High-Press Sodium Growing Lights

  - This light is good all-round and is especially good for seedlings as it has a red spectrum and the visible light is amber or orange.

- Metal Halides

  - These are the perfect grow room light as they emit a white or blue light that is closer to natural daylight and fluorescent lights. They are great for speeding up and ensuring a healthy growth rate for plants and seedlings.

T5 Growing Light

The T5 light is another light that is very good for growing healthy plants and seedlings. It is similar to fluorescent lighting but is a lot more efficient. It is a full spectrum light that is perfect for any type of indoor growing situation. This light is the closest light to emulating daylight as you are going to get.

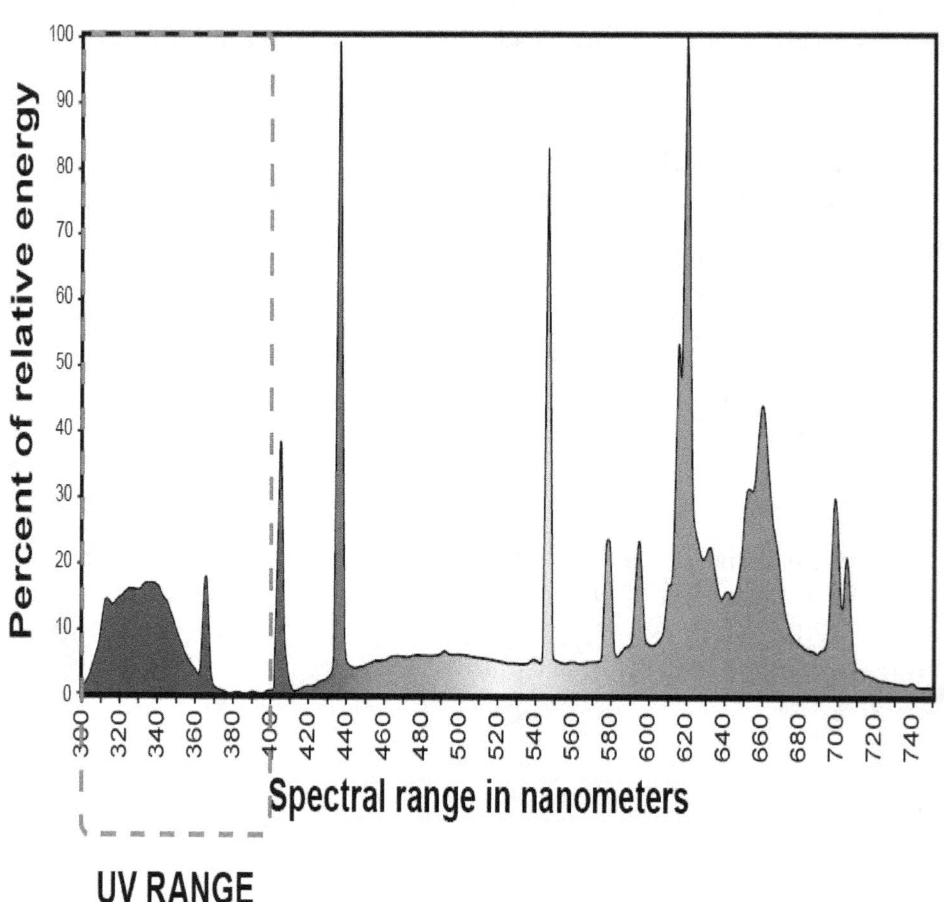

Chapter 5: How to Maintain a Hydroponic Garden

Hydroponic gardens need to have the proper care and maintenance, or they will not produce healthy plants. Not only do they need to be constantly cleaned, but there are various maintenance checks that need to be carried out in order to make sure the system remains functioning correctly.

A faulty drain, or a leaky pipe or switch could do serious damage to a hydroponic garden as most of the systems rely on their equipment and parts to work smoothly.

Cleanliness

In order to stop the build-up of algae, mold, and fungus or to stop attracting pests, keep the growing room as clean as possible.

Equipment should be flushed and cleaned at least twice a month to maintain water levels, stop algae growth, and ensure that there are no pests lurking about the system.

In order to stop pests and various fungal growth, growers should always make sure their hands are clean. Hands should be kept washed especially after handling anything that was dirty or in contact with a harmful substance.

Do not let old fallen leaves, stems, fruit, produce or growing media or even pots or discarded trays lie around the growing areas. Rather throw out any debris or broken items, and wash and pack away any unused equipment.

Wash all equipment after use and only reuse a growing medium if it can be reused and it has been thoroughly washed and sterilized. In fact, all growing mediums, whether old or new, should be thoroughly washed before being used as not to contaminate the grow pots, grow trays, and the reservoir.

Keeping the growing area and equipment clean cuts down on the chances of infestation and development of frustrating diseases that are a nuisance to get rid of.

Nutrient Solution

The proper nutrient solution for the plant type and system type should be used at the correct ratio of solution to water.

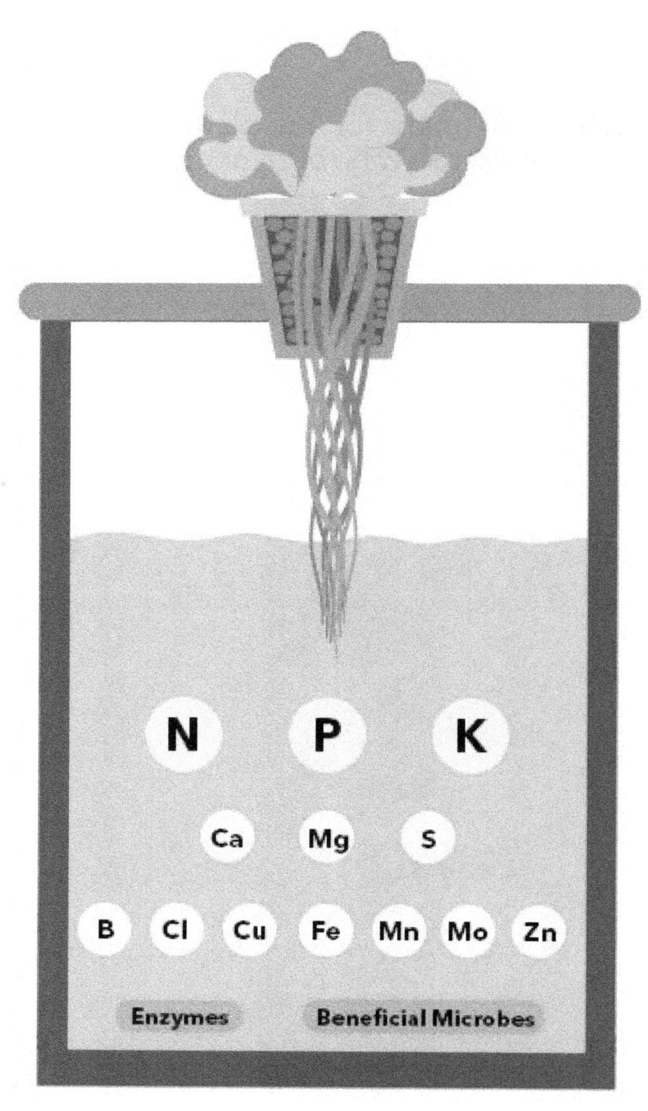

N
P
K
Ca
Mg
S
B
Cl
Cu
Fe
Mn
Mo
Zn
Enzymes
Beneficial Microbes

Only use good quality nutrient solutions with an organic base. Advance nutrients are only required should there be a problem that needs to be fixed, such as a nutrient deficiency in a plant.

The nutrient solution balance should be checked on a regular basis especially is it is a recovery system where the solution is being continuously recycled.

Make sure that the solution is flushed and completely refreshed on a regular basis and that there is no salt buildup, since this is very acidic and toxic to the plants.

Watering

Watering is done in many different ways and is delivered to each of the hydroponic systems differently.

Make sure the water is always fresh and checked on a regular basis. Algae is a common problem, as is nutrient build up in the system. An oxygen pump should be installed in order to ensure the water is being well hydrated and to keep the water fresher for longer.

Water solutions can come from the tap, drain systems, or rain collection tanks.

Watering can be on a continuous flow basis or set by a timer that switches on and off at different intervals during the day.

If possible, a person should always have a backup water solution available in case of an emergency and their primary watering source is unavailable. Some plants are very sensitive to their watering schedule and even a few minute's downtime and a missed watering schedule can cause some damage.

Reservoir Temperature

The water in the reservoir should be around 65 to 75 degrees Fahrenheit, which is basic room temperature. Water that is either too hot or too cold can damage the plant's root systems and their leaves.

The reservoir should be topped off with water in order to keep pH and nutrient levels constant. Change out the water on a regular basis.

Humidity

Different plants and hydroponic systems need the humidity to be on different levels. There are thermometers that can measure the humidity and temperature to ensure that the plants are comfortable. Keeping an optimum level does not encourage the growth of unwanted diseases and fungi.

Make sure plants that love the hotter temperatures get enough humidity by giving them a regular misting spray. This will help to keep the humidity constant for the plants that do not like too much humidity.

Inspect the Equipment

The equipment should be thoroughly inspected on a regular basis.

There are a lot of things that can go wrong in a hydroponic system, especially with the equipment. And the best way to troubleshoot is to try to avoid as many equipment malfunctions as possible.

The best way to inspect equipment it to keep the entire system in mind. When doing the inspection start at one point and work your way through your system.

Start with the reservoir and all the systems that are dependent on it.

- Water feeding pipe

  - This should be thoroughly checked for crimps that may not be feeding the solution correctly.

  - Nutrients build up in the pipes so they may need a thorough flushing out or replacing.

○ Check for any blockages in the pipe.

○ Check for any holes or leaks that could deter the flow of water pressure in the pipe.

○ Check for any algae or mold that may be growing in or around the pipe.

○ Determine if it may be time to replace the hoses.

○ Give them a good cleaning if they are still viable.

• Nozzles and hoses

○ Check the nozzles that feed the root systems, sprinklers, or misting systems.

○ When last were they changed?

○ Check for blockages or leakage.

○ Check any joins and washers for leaks.

○ Check for sediment build up, algae, or mold growing in or around these attachments.

○ Give them a good cleaning if they are still usable.

● Drain siphons and hoses

○ Check the drain pipes for blockages

○ When last were they replaced?

○ Check for leaks.

○ Check for algae or mold growing in or around these pipes.

○ They may need to have a good cleaning as part of the system maintenance.

● Check the reservoir water pump

○ Test the pump

○ Make sure it is still working correctly and pumping the water at the optimum flow.

○ Check that all pump attachments are not leaking air.

● Check the reservoir

○ Check that there is no build-up, algae, or mold growing on the reservoir.

○ Check for any leaks.

○ Make sure the water is at the optimum temperature for the hydroponic system and plants.

○ Check that any air pumps are functioning correctly and adequately oxygenating the tank.

○ Make sure any oxygen stones do not have unwanted algae or mold growth on them

- Growing trays

  ○ Make sure the growing tray(s) do not have any leaks in them.

  ○ Make sure the growing tray(s) are clean and have not unwanted algae or mold growing on them.

  ○ Clean off any nutrient build up and make sure the trays are clean.

  ○ For a closed system, the trays must be given thorough flushing out.

- Growing pots

  ○ Check that each of the pots is still intact and not broken.

○ Replace any that are not functioning correctly.

○ Make sure any growing medium is clean and does not have any unwanted algae or mold growing on them that could upset the plant's natural balance.

● Lighting equipment

○ Check that the bulbs are still functioning correctly.

○ Check that the lighting is still adequate for the environment.

○ Check the timers are working correctly.

○ Clean any residue off the lighting system.

- Temperature

  o Make sure that any thermostat is working correctly, and that room temperature is normal.

  o Check that the humidity is correct for the growing environment.

  o Check both the temperature and humidity thermometers to ensure that they are still working correctly.

- Ventilation

  o Make sure that there is adequate ventilation in the growing room.

○ Not enough ventilation can cause mold.

○ Check that all fans and cooling systems are working correctly.

• Support Systems

○ Check that any hanging supports for the plants are working without causing the plant or system any undue stress.

○ Make sure that the environment in which the hydroponic system is housed offers the correct infrastructure for the system to function correctly.

○ Make sure the plants are all supported and planted correctly to ensure a successful infrastructure.

• Tools

○ Are all the gardening tools in working order?

○ Are they cleaned?

○ Are there any that may need to be replaced?

Look at Your Plants

Make sure you keep a vigilant check on your growing plants. Measure their growth rate, root growth and when they are ready to harvest.

This gives a person a good measure of how the next batch should perform and something by which to determine if the growing medium, solution, or systems structure may need to be changed or optimized.

The plants must also be checked to make sure they are getting enough nutrients, they are growing as they should, and there are no pests or other infestations. A lot of growing problems and deficiencies can be caused by various infestations. Some are easy to spot, others may take more of an experienced eye, but as a gardener gets to know their plants they will come to instinctively know when something is wrong.

Look for the signs in seedlings such as slow growth , looking sad and droopy, white fluffy stuff growing on the leaves, etc.

Take the time to look over the plants; do not just rush through it. If there are a lot of plants to look over, break them into sections and do a revolving sweep of one section on this day, and the next section on another.

If there is an outbreak, you will need to go through the entire growing area right away.

Spending time with the plants in a hydroponic environment can also be quite good for the mind and spirit. Plants and running water are rather therapeutic and can reduce stress, anxiety and ease tension.

Change One Thing at a Time

If you are wanting to change or expand your system, do not try and do it all at once.

Choose a section to change, switch it around, or upgrade and start with that.

Before rushing out and buying expensive parts, why not try a bit of DIY and try to make it yourself. Or at least look around to see what you have available before rushing off to spend more money on an item you do not really need.

Hydroponic systems are not only flexible and versatile in what they can grow or how they deliver their solutions, but they can also be easily adapted to suit the grower's needs and lifestyle.

There are so many great DIY ideas on how to create the perfect hydroponic garden online these days that it is well worth a try. The money you save building the system yourself can be better spent on plants, growing media, or nutrient solutions.

In order to keep a system simple and working for you, think carefully about an upgrade or addition. Plot it out and then work through one section at a time getting that part right before moving on to the next.

Chapter 6: Common Problems and Troubleshooting

Every system even a well-run hydroponic system can have a few problems whether technical or with the plants. This can be anything from algae build-up to a faulty switch on a pump.

Here are a few common problems to consider:

Nutrient Deficiencies

One of the most important aspects of watering plants in a hydroponic environment is that the nutrient levels must be just the right balance for the plants they are nourishing. An imbalance can cause a number of problems for the plants.

To ensure that the plants are getting what they need, an advanced nutrient solution of good quality should be used. Make sure that the pH levels stay in the range of 5.8 to 6.3 and the nutrient EC levels are not lower than 1.2 or higher than 2.0.

When plants are in the soil, they find the nutrients they need and do this by extending their roots out to find a mineral source. In hydroponic gardens, there is no soil and the roots only support system is a non-nutritious growing medium. They rely solely on the nutrient solution mix that is being fed directly to their roots.

Although the roots may be getting fed various nutrients in a well-mixed water-nutrient solution, it may not be the right solution for that particular plant. In a mixed plant environment, this can happen because what one plant type is happy with another may not be. Just like how one person may need a little extra of this vitamin while another is okay without. The good thing about most of the nutrient solutions for hydroponics is that you can find one that will suit all your plants. The trick is to know what to look for in your current plants to determine what it is they may be lacking.

There are a few ways to diagnose certain nutrient deficiencies:

Boron Deficiencies

- The younger leaves are the first to be affected by a boron deficiency.

- The young leaves of the plant start to turn yellow.

- A boron deficiency will stunt the plant's growth.

- Any flowering buds will die without opening.

- The roots of the infected plant will be stunted and deformed.

- The overall appearance of the plant looks like it has been scorched.

Check the pH and EC levels of the nutrient solution. If they are fine and there are other like plants not affected it may be the positioning of the plant. Move it to a more prominent position and then try adjusting the nutrients to ensure that all plants are getting the correct nutrient intake.

If it is not the positioning of the plant, try changing the nutrient solution.

Calcium Deficiency

- Younger leaves are affected first.

- The new leaf tip, leaf edges, and inner parts of the leaf have brown patches on them.

- The leave tips are a bit distorted.

- The stems will have some black patches on them.

- The young leaf will die off and not last very long.

- Excessive buildup of calcium in a plant will stunt the plant's growth.

- The plant will have problems taking potassium and magnesium which in turn will cause more problems.

The only way to counteract this deficiency is to adjust the nutrient solution or use one with advanced nutrients in it. Keep the pH and EC levels at an optimum and remove any affected leaves.

Cobalt Deficiencies

- Cobalt is needed in plants as it is the bridge that allows them to take in other nutrients such as nitrogen and various metals.

- The younger leaves get affected first and will appear light green, almost a pale yellow, due to chlorosis.

This is a very rare deficiency but if it does happen, check the tank for various algae build up. It may be time to refresh the reservoir water. Try a new advanced nutrient solution and ensure that the water to nutrient ratio is correct.

Copper Deficiency

- The younger leaves will start to turn beige as chlorosis sets in.

- Leaf tips will curl and be malformed.

- The plant will suffer from an irregular growth rate.

- Too much copper is just as poisonous to a plant and if this happens, check for acidity in the nutrient solution.

Clean up the toxicity levels in the nutrient solution and the nutrient solution levels should be adjusted.

Iron Deficiency

- This is one of the most common deficiencies in plants and shows up a lot in plants that are grown indoors.

- Young leaves have darker leaf veins while the middle of the leaf has a yellow tinge to it.

- Younger leaves are a lot smaller than the older ones.

- Iron problems tend to occur when the water solution starts to turn acidic.

Check the pH levels and either clean out the tank or add more clean water to bring the levels back to normal.

Magnesium Deficiency

- Older leaves will get affected first.

- The outline of the leaf starts to turn dark and the discoloration will make its way towards the middle of the leaf.

- Discoloration starts to turn the leaf white in places, and it will eventually die.

The only way to counteract a magnesium deficiency in a hydroponic system is to augment the nutrients with an advanced calcium/magnesium solution.

Manganese Deficiency

- Young leaves will get affected first.

- The young leaves start to take on a wrinkled effect with mottled veins.

- Discoloration starts to turn the leaf white in places, and it will eventually die.

The deficiency of manganese comes from the root zone usually because the pH levels in the water nutrient solution have risen to well over 6.8. Bring the pH levels down and clear off the dead leaves.

Nitrogen Deficiency

- Older leaves will get affected first.

- The older leaves will start to take on a wrinkled effect with mottled veins.

- Discoloration starts to turn the leaves yellow and it will eventually die.

- Older plants can naturally lose nitrogen when near the end of their life span.

- If nitrogen is in excess, it will turn the leaves a darker green than normal. Excessive nitrogen affects the plant's ability to absorb nutrients and will dehydrate them.

Any form of nitrogen upset will cause plant harm. Check the pH levels of the reservoir are within the optimum range and used advanced nutrient products to counteract either a deficiency or excess.

Phosphorus Deficiency

- Older leaves will get affected first.

- The older leaf will start curl backward.

- The plant's growth rate will slow down and they will become spindly.

To adjust phosphorus levels, you will have to use advanced nutrients. Check the pH balance of the nutrient solution as well as the EC levels. The tank may need a complete cleanout and fresh solution.

Potassium Deficiency

- Older leaves will get affected first.

- The older leaf will start to go yellow and brown giving it a scorched look.

- If the plant is flowering, buds will fall off prematurely and die.

- Plants are stunted and the growth rate slows down.

The only way to augment potassium deficiency is with an advanced nutrient solution added to the nutrient mix.

Infestations

Infestations happen by way of pests and diseases. These are especially common on indoor grown plants.

Common Diseases:

- Algae

This usually grows on the growing media of the plant but can start to creep up on the plant itself. It is a thick green colored gooey mess. Although not a great threat it is still an indication that there is something not right with your growing environment.

Clean out all vents, change growing media and clean pumps, filters, etc. Change the reservoir water.

- Damping Off

This disease mainly affects seedlings where their growing media is far to damp. Damping off is fatal to the new plant and there is no way to cure it. Once it has attacked the seedling the plant will die. The root of the infected seedling looks like it is waterlogged.

You can prevent the disease by making sure that the media used to house the seedlings is fast draining and sterile. Make sure the seedling cubes are not kept too moist and they are properly drained.

• Downy Mildew

This is not to get confused with powdery mildew. It is a white substance that appears on the upper surface of the leaf, making it look like it has been burned by a cigarette.

Mildew is caused by damp conditions from the humidity in a growing area especially an indoor one. It can usually be wiped away, although it is best to get a non-toxic cleanser from a local nursery to clean the spores away. To discourage mildew, clean away dead leaves, old flowers, produce, etc.

• Gray Mold

This looks like fine cobwebs or silvery hair that usually extends from the leaves of the plant. It is quite common on tomatoes and is caused by too much humidity. Gray mold is not an outbreak you want, once it takes hold it can be quite devastating to the growing environments. and should be caught as early as possible.

Wipe away all the mold that can be found with a soft cloth, making sure to remove every bit of it. Remove all fallen leaves, old flowers, discolored leaves, etc. Each plant in the grow room will have to be thoroughly checked to ensure there is no mold on it.

The entire grow room should be thoroughly cleaned. The humidity in the room will need to be decreased and the air inflow increased.

- Powdery Mildew

Powdery mildew looks just like it sounds as if spots of powder have been dropped on the plant's leaves.

It is caused by high humidity, dampness, and not enough light.

The way to treat it is to decrease the humidity, increase the air circulation in the room and clear off the infected leaves. Make sure there is sufficient lighting for the plants. If there is too much, a fungicide may have to be considered.

- Root Rot

Root rot is when the roots get infected by a pathogen that chokes the roots and makes them become a slimy mess. Because the roots are not performing properly, the plant's growth slows and becomes stunted.

The plants themselves will start to turn yellow as they will be starved of nutrients. As the roots start to rot and decay, the plant will wither and die.

Change out the nutrient solution and clean the tank reservoir, pump and pump tubing. Completely clean out the hydroponic system and check all the plants in the infected grow area. Plants that are dying should be taken out of the rooms and those that can be saved must have their roots thoroughly drained and any dead or rotting roots removed.

The only way to clear root rot is to completely flush the entire hydroponic system.

- Wilts

Wilts affect plants like tomatoes, eggplants, and peppers. It causes small spots on the plant's leaves which eventually makes them start to curl up and dry out.

You will notice the leaves of the produce have browned, hardened, curled and dried out.

The only way to cure this disease is to get rid of the infected plants and completely flush out the hydroponic growing environment. Clean out all the dead plants and any debris around the room.

Common Pests:

• Aphids

These are commonly known as plant lice. They are either green, grey, or brown in color. They suck all the sap out of the plant's leaf and stem causing it severe damage. An attack of these critters will first show as the leaves start to turn yellow. They like to gather in a colony at the stem of the plant.

Aphids will need some form of organic pesticides to get rid of them. To prevent another attack, it may be beneficial to apply something like Rhino Skin.

• Fungus Gnats

The larvae of the fungus gnat are what attacks and destroy the plant. The adult gnat is not harmful to the plant. The larvae however can cause the plant's growth to slow, which can cause a bacterial infection and the death of the plant.

Sticky traps placed at the soil level of the plant will trap the gnats. The best cards for fungus gnats are the yellow ones. Once again, an organic trap is the best solution to kill off the larvae.

• Spider Mites

These are teeny little arachnids that are so small that they usually go unnoticed until they have caused major damage and increased their populations. The only sure way to spot if a plant has been infested with these mites is to look out for a fine webbing.

These are nasty little critters to try and get rid of but not impossible. It is going to take an organic pesticide. But the plant will have to be constantly monitored until all the eggs and any new hatchlings have been dealt with.

• Thrips

Thrips are tiny little insects that love to suck plants dry of their juice. Like the spider mite they are so tiny they are hard to spot. The only real way will be when the leaves on the infected plant start to get a metallic, black looking spot on the top of the leaf. Soon thereafter it will turn brown and wither up as the thrip sucks the leaf dry.

An organic pesticide will have to be used and the plants leaves wiped down. Any leaves that have the metallic spot must be plucked. Keep checking the rest of the plants in the grow room to ensure that all the thrips have been taken care of.

- Whiteflies

Whiteflies are really annoying and look like very small moths. Because they can fly, they tend to be quite hard to get rid of. Once you disturb a plant they are on, they will fly off to the next one. They breed and can spread at an alarmingly fast rate.

Once again organic pesticides and sticky traps are the keys to getting rid of these flies. Keep an eye on the plants and make sure to continue the application for a while after the first infestation has been taken care of. You do not want to miss any larvae that may have been left behind as this will quickly start another infestation

Seedling Problems

Like any new life, seeds are at their most vulnerable in the first few days to weeks of their life.

There are a few common seedling problems in hydroponic growing. In order to be able to respond quickly to them these little guys need you to check on them every day and keep an eye out for the following signs of a problem:

Seedlings do not Grow

- Most fresh seeds will grow without a problem. If a seed has been stored for longer than six months or so there is a good chance that it may not grow. This is because the older a seed gets, the less germination rate it has.

If a fresh seed, however, does not germinate there may be a problem with the growing medium or nutrient solution.

The best way to get a seed that has low germination to grow is to soak it for half a minute in a bit of water. This will soften the seed and help it to absorb moisture and encourage it to grow. Once the seed has been softened put into a grow block and make sure it has enough water but not too much as to drown it.

- The seedling has a spindly stem and the leaves are too small

This is due to seedlings trying to stretch towards the light and means that they are not getting enough direct light.

If you are using artificial grow lights, try to place the seedlings closer to the light. But be careful not to place them too close to the light as that will be just as damaging for the tender plants.

- The stems and leaves are all droopy

This is a classic sign of overwatering. The plant needs to dry out a little and the roots need some air.

Make sure the pot is not too big for the plant and make sure the growing medium is not holding too much moisture for the little plant.

- The leaves have yellow streaks and are pale

If, after a few days, the seedling suddenly stops growing and the leaves turned yellow and streaky, it means the little plant is lacking in nitrogen.

To begin correction a nitrogen deficiency in a seedling you will have to wait for it to produce at least two cotyledon leaves. Once these appear mix some nitrogen-rich advanced seedling solution in with their nutrient mix. It must be properly diluted following the manufacturer's specification in order to correct the deficiency.

- Leaves are curled and drying up

The seedlings are not getting enough water and nutrients. Seedlings need to be watered constantly and even one missed watering session can cause them damage.

Another cause of curled dried up leaves could be that the seedlings have too much heat on them from something like a grow light. Or they are positioned where there is too much direct sunlight.

Keep the plants cool and in a growing medium that retains just enough moisture to ensure the seedling has a constant supply of moisture to keep them from dehydrating.

- Leaves are purple or red

Newly developing plants need a lot of nutrients and a lack of them will cause the leaves to start to discolor. When the leaves of a seedling turn purple or red, it means the plant is lacking phosphorus.

The nutrient solution pH should be tested, and a correct balance established. If the nutrient solution is not ideal or too acidic, the little plant will not be able to absorb the nutrients it desperately needs to grow and thrive.

- Leaf tips are brown or yellow

If the room temperature is too warm the seedling will get too hot and will start to lose moisture as they overheat.

An ideal temperature setting for seedlings is around 65 degrees Fahrenheit.

Common System and Environmental Problems

Algae

Algae is not something that can be avoided when there is water involved. Especially when there is water mixed with nutrients and lighting. Although algae in itself is not the biggest problem and is not that hard to get rid of, it is quite a sneaky substance and at times things can go amiss.

Algae attracts the unwanted attention of pests such as fungus gnats and other nasty critters and growths. There are ways to try and prevent algae buildup such as:

- Use darker materials for the reservoir and try to limit the nutrient's exposure to direct light.

- The holes that feed the nutrient and drainage pipe should be just big enough to fit them through.

- These pipes should be made from materials that do not expose the water traveling through them to direct light.

- Check the plant baskets and growing medium regularly for any algae growth.

- Try to cap off any holes that may expose the solution to direct light that could attract the unwanted attention of algae.

System Leaks

- Hydroponic systems are prone to some leaks, especially the high-pressure systems.

- The biggest source of most of these leaks is usually at join points such as stab fittings, t-joints, and sprinkler systems.

- This could be due to:

○ The stab holes being slightly too big for the fitting.

- o The joints not being pushed incorrectly for the hose or cap fittings.

- o The fittings not being the correct size for the piece it is meant to join.

Systems getting Clogged

- Pumps can get clogged.

- Pipes can get clogged.

- Plant baskets can get clogged.

- Sprinkler or spray systems can get clogged.

- Some growing medium such as coco coir is known for clogging drainage systems.

Incorrect Humidity

Hydroponic systems often have problems with incorrect humidity. This is something that can go wrong at any time. A heater or cooling system could malfunction, or a spray timer could be set incorrectly.

There are many factors that could cause a humidity problem and like algae, humidity problems have a knock-on effect. If not caught in time they can lead to other problems:

- Low humidity can cause leaf burn.

- High humidity is the perfect environment for various nasty fungi to grow.

- It can cause glassiness, edema, and tip burn.

Most crops are comfortable at a 70 to 75 % humidity.

Issues with Various Gases

One of the most overlooked pieces of equipment in indoor plant growing is a carbon dioxide monitor. This is needed in order to keep the various gases at levels that are both safe and acceptable to humans and plants.

- For an optimum carbon dioxide enriched environment, the levels should be in the range of 600 to 1,200 ppm.

- It is very important to ensure that there is a carbon dioxide monitor and that it is always working in growing houses.

- High levels of carbon dioxide in a grow house is toxic to the grower and can cause a person to lose coordination, become dizzy and pass out. Carbon Dioxide levels in the hydroponic growing houses should never get to levels in rangers of 5000 ppm.

- Carbon Dioxide poisoning to plants mimics a few nutrient deficiencies which it can easily be mistaken for. These include curling and browning of the leaves, yellowing and chlorosis, stunted plant growth and necrosis.

Chemical issues

Although Hydroponics does not use any actual chemicals, the plants can still be affected by chemicals from the nutrients supplied. This usually ends up being something to do with the quality or composition of the nutrient solution used.

For instance, tomato plants are not as susceptible to salt build up as cucumbers are. If cucumbers are exposed to too much sodium their leaves will get a yellow band around them. This could also be caused by the use of the city water supply, as certain chemicals used to treat city water can affect nutrient solutions.

Keeping a good chemical balance is not the easiest of things to do when running a system that is reliant on a water soluble nutrient system. The best water to use is that of rain runoff into actual catchment tanks that have not had any type of chemical treatments.

General System Problems

Troubleshooting any system can be complex as there are many factors that can influence both the problem and solution, especially in a system that has so many moving parts that need to work together in balanced harmony to give the desired outcome.

A well maintained and monitored system will ensure that most of the working parts function at their optimum. Although it is not always feasible it is always a good plan to have a backup of the main parts like a spare pump, filter, fittings, and pipes.

That way the system downtime is not as long and there is a good chance that there will be no damage to the plants.

Conclusion

Hydroponics is an economical, environmentally friendly way to grow plants and produce without soil or pesticides. The plants grow faster and produce bigger yields while being completely GMO-free, making them a lot healthier to eat.

Not only does hydroponics allow for fast, efficient, cost effective growing environments, but it is a means to grow produce where it otherwise was not able to grow. Thanks to innovative irrigation systems and the use of various growing media, places that have inadequate soil composition are able to grow fresh produce.

Hydroponics also provides a growing solution for places that have little to no space for commercial growing lands. It has even been successfully tested in space. Hydroponics is not a new concept but has come a long way since ancient times and keeps moving forward in leaps and bounds with new methods being introduced along the way.

It is not a hard concept to grasp and some methods are really easy to learn. There are ready-made kits that one can buy and assemble for each type of system. But they are all capable of being homemade with materials found around the home.

Hydroponics is a great way to teach children the joy of gardening without the mess of dirt and as the plants grow relatively quickly it holds their attention better than normal gardening does.

There are many exciting growing opportunities to be had with hydroponics and if done right, you will be rewarded with bountiful, healthy crops.

Aquaponics adds another dynamic level to the sustainable green farming in that it utilizes natural nutrients generated from a fish tank to organically nourish a media bed. In turn, the media beds offer the fish tank clean water as they filter out all the waste products and return clean water to the fish tank.

Many definitions of aquaponics recognize the 'ponics' part of this word for hydroponics which is growing plants in water with a soil-less media. Hydroponics is its own growing technique with execs and cons (discussed later).

Literally speaking, Aquaponics is putting fish to work. It with great care happens that the work those fish do (eating and manufacturing waste), is that the good chemical for growing plants. And man, fish will grow tons of plants once they get to work!

One of the coolest things about Aquaponics is that it mimics a natural ecosystem. Aquaponics represents the relationship between water, aquatic life, bacteria, nutrient dynamics, and plants which grow together in waterways all over the world. Taking cues from nature, aquaponics harnesses the power of bio-integrating these individual components: Exchanging the waste by-product from the fish as a food for the bacteria, to be converted into an ideal chemical for the plants, to return the water in a clean and safe form to the fish. Just like mother nature will in each aquatic system.

Traditional Soil Gardening

Soil can be a wonderful natural resource, or a very time-consuming element to manage when you are trying to grow plants.

Some soils have robust fertile live soil-web ecosystems. However many soil structures that are heavy in clay or sand have challenges related to water, nutrient availability and texture for planting.

Many locations lack soil access because they have concrete, asphalt or rock to contend with.

Along with water runoff, erosion, wind and other soil depleting events, soil loses fertility with each crop. To grow plants in soil, it is necessary to reapply compost or some other fertilizer each growing season. Fertilizers with only N – P – K (Nitrogen, Phosphorus and Potassium), means that the plants grown will absorb these nutrients, but could be depleted of other micro-nutrients such as calcium, boron, copper, iron, zinc, and many others. Applying too much synthetic fertilizer or uncomposted manure can create salinity issues rendering the soil "too hot" to grow crops.

Managing weeds, pests, insects and diseases takes a significant amount of the gardener or farmers time. Weeds crowd plants, taking water and nutrients, not to mention all the time wasted killing or pulling them out. Pesticides, herbicides and other chemicals can also kill precious soil microbes and can be dangerous to bees, butterflies, birds, other animals, and humans.

In large scale industrial farming, agrochemicals (fertilizers, pesticides, and herbicides) along with Genetically Modified Organisms (GMOs) are of concern when choosing vegetables, fruits, and herbs. Organically grown crops do not allow GMOs but do have a wide variety of products used for pesticides.

Soil can be very difficult to water correctly. Overwatering can result in flooding, evaporation, runoff, soil compaction, prevent air to get to the roots and kill plants with saturation. Alternatively, insufficient water, hot dry climates, drought and water shortages will hinder optimal plant growth and may simply lead to plant death yet.

Gardening can be an enjoyable past-time but also demands a certain amount of digging, bending, and physical labor

While gardens can be located in your backyard. Industrial farms are often thousands of miles from where their food is consumed. This requires extensive transportation, refrigeration, and packaging to get the food from farm to table.

Traditional Hydroponics

Traditional farming systems settle for the careful application of expensive, synthetic nutrients made from a combination of concocted chemicals, salts and trace components. In aquaponics, you merely feed your fish with inexpensive fish feed, food scraps, and food you grow yourself.

The strength of this farming mixture must be fastidiously monitored, along with pH and total dissolved solids (TDS). In aquaponics, you fastidiously monitor your system throughout the first month, but once your system is established you only need to check the pH and ammonia levels weekly or if your plants or fish seem stressed.

Water in farming systems must be discharged sporadically, as the salts and chemicals build up in the water, becoming toxic to the plants. This is both inconvenient and problematic as the disposal location of this wastewater needs to be carefully considered. In aquaponics, you do not need to replace your water; you only top it off as it evaporates.

Hydroponic systems area unit is vulnerable to a sickness known as "Pythium" or plant disease. This disease is virtually non-existent in aquaponics.

Recirculating Aquaculture

Most mainland fisheries are Recirculating Aquaculture Systems, or RAS, which tries to filter and re-use fish tank water. While RAS will conceive to address conservation, it also comes with its own issues

The tank water becomes impure with fish effluent, giving off high concentrations of ammonia. Water must be discharged at a rate of 10-20% of the whole volume within the tank daily. This uses a tremendous amount of water. Again, in associate aquaponics system, discharging your water becomes unnecessary.

This water is usually pumped-up into open streams wherever it pollutes and destroys waterways.

Because of this unhealthy setting, fish area unit becomes vulnerable to sickness and area unit will often require treatment with medicines, including antibiotics. Fish disease is rare in an aquaponics system.

Aquaponics

Aquaponics uses the best of all the growing techniques, utilizing the waste of one element to benefit another in a way that mimicks a natural ecosystem. It's a game changer

Waist-high aquaponic agriculture eliminates weeds, back strain, and small animal access to your garden.

Aquaponics depend on the use of nutrient-rich water unceasingly. In aquaponics, there is no toxic run-off from either hydroponics or aquaculture.

Aquaponics uses 1/10th of the water of soil-based agriculture and even less water than farming or recirculating cultivation.

No harmful petrochemicals, pesticides or herbicides can be used. It's a natural ecosystem.

Gardening chores are cut down dramatically or completely eliminated. The aquaponics granger is ready to specialize in the pleasant tasks of feeding the fish and tending to as well as harvesting the plants.

Aquaponic systems can be placed anywhere; use them outside, in a greenhouse, in your basement, or in your living room. By victimization grow-lighting, an area can become a productive garden.

Aquaponic systems are scalable. They can match most sizes and budgets; from small countertop herb systems to backyard gardens, to full-scale farms, aquaponics can do it all.

And the better part – You get to reap each plants and fish from your garden. Truly raise your entire meal in your backyard!

Instead of victimization dirt or cytotoxic chemical solutions to grow plants, aquaponics uses extremely nourishing fish effluent that contains all the desired nutrients for optimum plant growth. Instead of discharging water, aquaponics uses the plants, in situ bacterium, and therefore the media within which they grow in to wash and purify the water, such that when it's returned to the fish tank, this water will be reused indefinitely and can only be topped-off once it's lost through transpiration from the plants and evaporation.

Chapter 1: What Is Aquaponics?

Aquaponics is essentially a system in which fish and plants work together so that both can thrive. The two are cultivated together by way of a system built that utilizes recirculation of its natural biological processes.

This ecological system involves waste production from the fish to be processed by bacteria and repurposed into necessary plant food that will then clean the water for the fish. Each plays a helping hand in the Aquaponics system that allows people to have an abundance of environmentally friendly, healthy, fresh food sources of both vegetation and fish. This system was born from the combination of the best parts of Hydroponics and Aquaculture, while removing the negatives associated with both, such as chemical additives for fertilization, the need for discarding water, and filtration.

History And Current Uses

Aquaponics may be on the rise in familiarity and use amongst both commercial farmers and home growers, but it is certainly not a new concept. We simply get the privilege of using the new and improved, and much easier versions of Aquaponics. As they say, history repeats itself, and those that are wise will learn from those before us. It will never cease to amaze me how centuries ago, before technology, before machinery, before mass communication and social networks, our ancestors were able to create such great inventions that allowed their people to not just survive but thrive, in many areas where the environment seemed to be a major impediment.

In some form or another, Aquaponics was used throughout the continent in places like China's rice paddy fields, in Africa, in Italy, throughout the islands, by Native Americans, and the Aztecs in Mexico, to name a few. The Aztecs migrated to an area that is known today as Mexico City.

The land there did not have good soil for farming and the inner areas were all marshes. In order to adapt to this unproductive environment, they created numerous rafts on the lake out of substances found in the area, such as reeds and mud. On the rafts, they made gardens that utilized the nutrients from the aquatic species in the water to feed the plants.

Back in the day when people lived off the land, (in some places, they still do), it was vital to observe nature, take its natural processes, and use it in all aspects of life. Because of these observations, we have Aquaponics today! It is also important to note that in third world countries - just like the Aztecs so many centuries ago - faced obstacles in their environment such as bad soil, lack of water, and many people were starving.

Many organizations are stepping in and introducing Aquaponics due to their fast-food growth without much water and soil-free gardening capabilities. In addition to a much-needed food source, it offers healthier, cleaner eating with much-needed vitamins and nutrients to aid in improving immune systems and fighting illness. The added bonus: Helping to prevent disease in one part of the world, stops the spread of disease to other parts of the world!

Chapter 2: Why Aquaponics?

The basic understanding of Organic is that the food was grown according to specific guidelines determined by the USDA that forbid the use of insecticides as well as requires strict adherence to the conservation of biodiversity and maintaining the welfare of animals. Essentially, this refers to the way Agriculture is raised and processed.

The regulations differ greatly in every country. United States' crops labeled organic needs to be raised free of synthetic pesticides, bioengineered genes (GMO's), and petroleum-based and sewage-based fertilizers. For livestock raised for the purpose of meat, eggs, or dairy products to be labeled as organic, they must have access to the outdoors for the majority of the day, daily. They must also be fed organic feed and cannot be administered any antibiotics, growth hormones, or any by-products of animals.

Additionally, if you choose to get locally grown food versus shipped organic, you are aiding the local economy. More money goes to the local farmer instead of to the expense of marketing, packaging, and distribution. In the U.S. alone, food will likely travel approximately 1500 miles and in order to maintain freshness during the trip, the produce is picked before it is ripe and will ripen during travels or the food is processed with preservatives or other processes in an effort to keep it from going bad prior to sale. This means that food purchased from local farmers will be fresh and have much more flavor.

By choosing to grow your own food at home, you are getting the benefits you would from both organic and locally grown and having the added benefit of saving money.

In order to fully grasp how immensely beneficial Aquaponics is and why you should use it, it is important to also know about its roots, Hydroponics and Aquaculture. By comparing the three different systems, understanding their purpose, and noting their advantages and disadvantages, you will have a much better idea of which system is best for you. I believe, that like myself, you will gain a deeper appreciation for what Aquaponics can do for you as a new home garden and fish cultivator and through experiencing Aquaponics, you may expand further either into business endeavors or into larger home systems.

Hydroponics

Hydroponics is a soil-free system of cultivating plants. In this system, the plants sit directly in the nutrient-rich water or are placed in soil free media such as gravel where the water can easily flow through. Once the nutrients have been used by the plants, it is necessary to add more nutrients or recycle the water.

Aquaculture

Aquaculture means water life and is, therefore, is a system of cultivating fish. This system is basically tanks or aquariums where fish can be bred and grown and requires constant filtration in order to maintain clean water where fish could live and thrive.

Aquaponics

Aquaponics is a system that combines Hydroponics and Aquaculture to cultivate both fish and plants together in one harmonious ecosystem. In Hydroponics, it is vital to recycle the water and add much-needed nutrients for the plants and in Aquaculture, it is vital to have water filtration for your aquatic species. By combining the two, Aquaponics removes the need to waste water, filtrate, and fertilize. Additionally, time and energy are reduced in the process.

It may just be the perfect marriage, but as in any marriage, there is some work involved in keeping everyone happy and healthy. In the end, it is all worth it. This union has created so many positives that make the negatives insignificant. In addition, it is outweighed by the benefits.

The following chart will show the benefits and drawbacks to all three:

Compare and contrast

Based on the chart provided, it is clear that there are pros and cons to all three and it really is up to the individual as to which system they prefer, but in my opinion there is really no reason to look anywhere else but to Aquaponics for my cultivation needs.

Hydroponics Pros and Cons

There is no soil needed in a hydroponics system. It produces fast growth of plants while making better use of space and location. Hydroponics is climate controlled so it, therefore, removes any seasonal barriers that one would experience in a regular garden or farm. You have complete control over what your plants eat because you have to feed them nutrient concoctions or chemical fertilizers daily. You have control over pH levels. There are no weeds because of the lack of soil and the use of insecticides removes the potential for pests.

On the flip side, chemical fertilizers may be great for your plant growth but they may not necessarily be safe for human ingestion and therefore a vigorous washing process must be undertaken. Hydroponics is time-intensive and requires daily monitoring. It is important to conduct system checks throughout the day because a system failure can be catastrophic to your production. Hydroponics is not easy on the wallet.

It can get quite expensive to maintain and the return on your investment may take quite a long while to occur. As mentioned before, pesticides may be used but would defeat the purpose of healthy produce so other measures would need to be taken to ensure pest control. If pests or diseases do show up, the spread in this type of environment can be extremely fast.

Aquaculture can be used as a source of food for both people and marine species. It is a source of income for many who provide fresh fish to fish markets and restaurants locally. It gives great flexibility to build fish farms, tanks, and cages anywhere. Systems created around the idea of recirculation help reduce, reuse, and recycle waste. Aquaculture has greatly reduced the strain on natural populations as fewer people are fishing and more people are breeding and raising the fish.

A major problem has occurred with the waste of water because many still have not incorporated recirculation into their Aquaculture setups. In addition to water waste, lack of recirculation would then waste valuable natural resources found in the water that is made by fish waste and waste of invaluable plant nutrient source.

Of course, there is also the argument about the propagation of invasive species and the threat to coastal ecosystems due to waste disposal and pollution. CDC states that this contaminates the water and threatens health.

An Aquaponics Garden using Deep Water Culture

Here are the seven advantages to having your own aquaponics system in your garden reception.

1. *Know the supply of your food*

Growing your own food offers you the additional advantage that you'll grasp precisely wherever and the way the food has been grown. you'll be able to choose the plants you wish to grow, and also the fish you wish to use within the tanks.

Some standard plants that are easy to grow in aquaponics setups include; unifoliate greens, herbs, tomatoes, peppers and cucumbers.

The fish you select to incorporate in your tank can depend on whether or not you wish to reap the fish, or have decorative seafood. If you wish to lift fish to eat, the foremost common selection is Tilapia.

2. *Reduces food miles*

More and a lot of individuals are beginning to ask questions on where their food is coming from and therefore the native food movement is absolutely growing as a lot of individuals who are beginning to query the carbon footprint of food miles.

Most of the food out there in supermarkets currently, includes a sizable quantity of air miles. It's seemingly the food can are mature lots of, perhaps even thousands of miles away, so flown into the native space.

With associate degree aquaponics system, you'll be able to supply the fish and plant seeds from a well-thought-of supply, and grow your own food right there in your back garden.

3. No chemicals

Another great thing about growing food in associate degree aquaponics system is that it's not possible to cheat and use chemicals or artificial fertilizers or pesticides.

Because one among the most elements during this created is live fish, if you add something that might hurt the fish to the system, you'll obviously kill them and therefore the whole setup won't work.

Therefore this method is one among the foremost organic and natural ways to grow food.

4. Uses relatively less water than other food farming strategies

Aquaponics uses up to ninetieth less water than the other ancient agricultural strategies.

This is as a result of ninety fifth of the water being reused. The water works in a very continuous closed-loop system system, passing through the plants that act as a filtration, improvement the water.

This removes the necessity to possess the do water changes as you'd do with regular cultivation, and additionally removes the necessity to water the plants.

5. Grow food in any sized area

As the world's population is growing, we'd like to seek out innovative ways in which to grow food in little places. Aquaponics fits this description.

Systems may be designed vertically, horizontally, stacked on prime of 1 another, just about any that thanks to use the obtainable area.

Whether you have got a small curtilage, or an oversized sprawling garden, you'll be able to style Associate in Nursing aquaponics system that you'll be able to grow food in.

6. *Sustainable food supply*

This methodology of growing food is crucial for variety of diverse reasons. It uses less water than alternative strategies as a result of it will ceaselessly recirculate the water. Soil is off from the equation which implies this method is feasible to use in areas that lack nutrient soils or sufficient water.

All the nutrients that the plants want come back from the fish, therefore it's a very natural fertilizing methodology. this method mimics the natural scheme, that means the plants ar mature organically, and therefore the quality of the food is way higher.

This methodology produces next to no waste. Any solids that ar left over within the fish tanks may be used as natural fertilizers for soil based mostly plants, or additional to the cumulus. Any unharvested or broken plants may be fed to the fish or composted.

7. Less time intensive than alternative agricultural *strategies*

If you've perpetually needed to grow your own food, however have perpetually been postpone by the thought of however long it's, then aquaponics could be a nice various.

Aside from have to be compelled to feed the fish daily, this method just about takes care of itself. You won't have to be compelled to water the plants, or flip any soil. Associate in Nursing aquaponics set-up is self-sustaining.

Chapter 3: The Master Plan Basics

It is important to determine what exactly you want to achieve with your Aquaponics system, how you want it to look, and where you want it to be located. Coming up with a plan is necessary to ensure that all pieces of the puzzle not only fit together but that there aren't any pieces missing.

No one likes working on a puzzle for hours only to find that they can't finish what they started. This project has many stages: planning stage, supply stage, building stage, and testing stage, plant and fish stages (don't occur at the same time), maintenance stage, and for some, the expansion stage. I personally enjoy the sit back and enjoy or feast stage and yet others are more concerned with reaping the reward. Whatever the desired outcome, a plan is vital.

Diy or kit

It is a matter of preference whether you choose to purchase a ready-made kit or do it yourself. Unless you happen to have a background in engineering or plumbing, I would strongly suggest that first time Aquaponics gardeners start with kits that are purchased from a very reputable company with knowledge and experience in Aquaponics.

I stress this point because there are many kits on the market that can be bought pretty much anywhere and if you purchase it online from say a company like Walmart or Amazon, you would not have the ability to talk to anyone with expertise in Aquaponics that can help you choose the right system for you and answer any questions you might have. Further, after you have the system set up, it is good to be able to contact the company for any advice or assistance you may need.

Your first kit is your opportunity to learn a great deal about Aquaponics as you are getting your feet wet. Purchasing a kit will remove much of the stress and allow you to enjoy what Aquaponics has to offer.

If you choose to jump right in with a DO IT YOURSELF project, there will be a lot of trial and error, research, shopping around for supplies, and no direct contact person to aid you as you venture on this Aquaponics mission.

If you are able to find a kit that suits your needs and your wallet, go for it! It will allow you to get started on the road to a bountiful harvest much quicker, without the worry of troubleshooting the do it yourself project. DO IT YOURSELF can delay production by several months. The initial cost of purchasing a kit is worth it when you save time and money in the long run.

DO IT YOURSELF can get expensive with the trial and error process one must endure plus you may not have all of the tools needed which is another purchase and of course the knowledge that is only gained over time to know exactly what supplies you need and which places are good to go (who you can trust) to get them from. Sometimes the simple task of purchasing supplies can be daunting because the Aquaponics supplies needed may not be easy to find. Kits come with everything you need to get started and are available for all sizes and levels of Aquaponics.

After you are used to Aquaponics and have a better understanding on how the system works and what it takes to be successful in Aquaponics, then you may choose to try your hand at a do it yourself project. Remember, Aquaponics is not for everyone and investing a lot of time and money in a do it yourself project initially doesn't make sense unless you are certain that Aquaponics is for you.

If you are an Aquaponics newbie and still choose to try your hand at a do it yourself project, you can buy excellent plans from reputable companies online and build it yourself. This would be the best option for DO IT YOURSELF Aquaponics first timers. If you have the time and skills, and choose the DO IT YOURSELF path, it can be significant savings for you. I pose the alternate point... If you attempt to DO IT YOURSELF and don't have the time and skills, you could end up spending considerably more as mentioned before.

Assuming that you chose to DO IT YOURSELF because you do have the time and skills, you have the distinct potential to customize the Aquaponics system to suit your needs and tastes. You will additionally benefit by gaining education about each part that you use to make your Aquaponics garden as you find out the intricacies of how they work and what they are needed for.

Basically, DO IT YOURSELF leaves room for your inner creative soul to flourish and for those who enjoy the challenge of recycling and reusing, this could be very rewarding.

For the purpose of introducing readers to the basics of Aquaponics and how to create your very own Aquaponics garden, chapter 6 will delve into what DIY supplies are recommended and the best ways in which to connect the two worlds of fish and plants.

Inside Or Out?

A matter of preference really, as Aquaponics can be done basically anywhere. It is for you to decide what is best for you and the Aquaponics goals you would like to achieve.

For those that desire an inside garden:

- You have the freedom to maintain the temperature in accordance with the needs of your plants and fish
- You must have grow lights
- Size and appearance are dependent on location
- You need to make sure that the location you select can withstand the weight of your system when the tank/aquarium is filled with water

For those that desire an outside garden:

- No soil is needed but an excellent lighted area is important

- Must have close proximity to a water source

- Must have connectivity to an outlet for electrical source

- Will your system be in a greenhouse or will it need protection such as a fence or netting to ward off pests?

- Dependent on the climate where you live, a heating system may be needed to maintain proper temperatures

Size and appearance

For me, appearance is important, so the setup of my system is very important in that regard. I do not want it to resemble an industrial zone. This is my home, so I want to find a compromise between décor and function.

Others may be more concerned with function and output and maybe with ease for productivity. Whatever your taste, putting the appearance aside, in Aquaponics, size does matter. It does not matter in barbaric terms of ah-hah mine is bigger than yours, but it does matter in regards to:

- What your ecosystem needs, in terms of ratios (example: plants to fish capacity)
- What your fish growth may be (remember, some fish like catfish get long and require much bigger tanks)
- Where your system is located (indoor area may not support large tanks)
- What you can afford overall (keep ongoing maintenance and utilities in mind)
- What your goals are (is this just a hobby? Is it just for ornamental purposes for both plants and fish? Or do you plan on expanding in the future?)

Plants and fish living together

It is highly recommended to use freshwater fish since saltwater fish will restrict which plants you can grow in your garden.

In addition to determining whether you want to eventually eat your fish you simply want fish for ornamental purposes, you will need to determine what plants you want to grow because this ecosystem needs good matchmaking in order for the marriage to last. It is important to know:

- Does your fish require warm water or cool water?
- Can your fish survive in both temperatures? A few can acclimate to both.
- How big will your fish get?
- How many plant beds do you plan on having?
- Do you want cool weather plants or warm weather plants? Or do you want seasonal plants?
- What size fish will you get? (Fish fry, Fingerlings, or Adult fish)
- What are your local laws? There are restrictions on the types of plants and fish you can grow in each area.

Fish like Catfish, Bluegill, (Food fish) Koi and Goldfish (Ornamental fish) are pretty resilient and adapts easily to different temperatures making them the most popular fish for both the fish for food and fish for ornamental categories. Other fish like Trout and Tilapia which are also very popular Aquaponics breeds have very specific temperature needs. Tilapia require warm water (above 70 degrees) while Trout require cooler waters falling below that temperature.

Likewise, Leafy Greens, peas, cabbage, carrots, beets and spinach require cooler temperatures. Beans, squash, and sweet corn require warmer temperatures while tomatoes, peppers, eggplant, and melon are all seasonal (summer vegetation).

In order for your ecosystem to align harmoniously, choosing which plant or fish that goes well together is of vital importance.

The following fish have had the best results in Aquaponics systems:

- Tilapia

- Bluegill/ Brim

- Sunfish

- Crappie

- Koi

- Fancy Goldfish

- Pacu

- Ornamental Fish: Tetras, Angelfish, Mollies, Guppies, and Swordfish

These fishes are also popular Aquaponics fish that do well but may require more work:

- Carp

- Barramundi

- Silver Perch

- Yellow Perch

- Catfish

- Large Mouth Bass

- Cod (Murray, Sleepy)

- Salmon

- Rainbow Trout

- Minnows

It is important to note that nearly all freshwater fish are edible. The difference in each would be how easy it is to prepare, the taste, and health. Koi and Goldfish are not suggested as edible simply because they are known to carry cancer-causing factors that affect humans.

Another important determination is the size and age of the fish. Though the cost may be a big determining factor, it is important to note:

- Fish fry is cheaper, but it will take much longer to mature and thus will affect the nitrate production levels, taking longer to reach adequate supply needed for the plants to absorb.

- Fingerlings are expensive, but for good reason. They are ideal for waste production in early stages which results in expedited vegetable growth.
- Mature fish are the most expensive to purchase and cannot be mixed with fish fry as they will be eaten by the larger of the species. Additionally, larger fish require more plant beds and larger tanks.

Important to note: For a 100-gallon fish tank with a 100 gallon grow bed, the proper amount of fish would be about 12 to 15 pounds. The correct ratio would be one pound of fish for every square foot of grow bed volume, which amounts to approximately seven and a half gallons, if and only if you properly circulate the entire volume of water in the tank every hour on the hour.

When you harvest your own fish for the purpose of eating it as opposed to purchasing your fish from the store, aside from the convenience, of course, you have the added reassurance that your fish is fresh and safe.

By raising the fish yourself, you have the distinct knowledge of what they eat and when it was harvested. You are the only one controlling every aspect of the environment, health, and growth of the fish which you consume. Additionally, the fact that they are cold blooded means that they are not susceptible to carrying harmful bacteria like E. Coli and Salmonella.

The Center for Disease Control (CDC) is always monitoring and stressing that people need to be aware of potential risks of fish consumption because contaminants (such as mercury or polychlorinated biphenyls) from pollution (coming from industry, houses, or simply people) in the lakes, oceans, and rivers, work their way into the fish that reside there.

This brings new meaning to "you are what you eat". By raising your own fish for consumption, you are removing any cause for concern because you know your fish are healthy.

Why is Fish consumption good for you? Fish that have white meat, more so than others, will have a lower fat content in comparison to other proteins sourced from animals. Fish that fall in the category of "oily fish", such as salmon, sardines, trout, mackerel, and bluefin tuna, are one of the best sources for good fats known as omega-3 fatty acids.

Our bodies do not naturally create these vital nutrients in the quantities we need so it is very important to incorporate these into our diet through other sources and fish are not only a perfect source but a delicious one too!

- One of the healthiest foods out there
- Great source of abundant nutrients, protein, and vitamins (many people are highly deficient in vitamin D and this is a great source for improving that deficiency)
- Omega-3 fatty acids are essential for body and brain and scientifically proven to reduce the risk of numerous

diseases. (They say an apple a day, keeps the doctor away, well a fatty fish or two a week, will give you all the omega-3 that your body requires).

- The fattier the fish, the better it is for us... super healthy!
- Whether you are pre-genetically disposed to heart attacks and/or strokes or you just want to do everything you can to avoid them (that would be all of us!), you can lower your risk of heart disease and other ailments simply by eating fish!
- Highly beneficial to children, fish contains DHA which helps development and growth.
- Researchers now state that eating fish regularly aids in the battle against deterioration in brain functions which tend to occur as people age. There is also evidence that grey matter of the brain is increased by consuming fish on a regular basis which would result in improved recollection and emotional status.
- Fish can not only make you healthier but studies have linked regular consumption to happiness and improvement in mental well-being.
- Source containing the highest level of vitamin D
- Fish is known to combat autoimmune diseases
- Studies show that when children consume fish regularly, it will help them combat asthma which will make it less likely to progress into adulthood
- Carrots are not the only thing recommended for eyesight. Fish has been studied in the battle against macular degeneration.
- Aside from the numerous health advantages linked to eating fish regularly, fish actually tastes amazing and comes in so many varieties. Fish is easy to prepare (for the most part) and there are so many recipes out there

that you could literally not eat the same meal twice within the same year if you wanted the variety.

- Fish does not take long to cook and therefore those people who don't have a lot of time to spend on cooking their meals, fish is a great option.

What kinds of plants work in aquaponics?

The most common plants for Aquaponics gardens are:

- Leafy lettuce
- Bok Choy
- Kale
- Spinach
- Swiss Chard
- Arugula
- Herbs such as Basil, Coriander, Sage, Lemongrass, Parsley, and Mint
- Watercress
- Chives
- Common Houseplants

Other plants that do well but are dependent on a well-stocked fish tank are:

- Tomatoes

- Peppers

- Cucumbers

- Beans

- Peas

- Squash

- Broccoli

- Cauliflower

- Cabbage

- Eggplant

- Melon

- Fruiting plants such as Strawberries

Others have noted success with:

- Bananas

- Citrus trees like limes, lemons, and oranges

- Pomegranate

- Sweet Corn

- Microgreens

- Beets

- Radishes

- Carrots

- Onions

- Shallots

- Chili peppers

- Capsicum

- Celery

- Ginger

- Edible Flowers like Orchids and Violas

Why are vegetables good for you? Aside from being naturally lower in fat and calories and a major source of vitamins, minerals, and nutrients, there are many health benefits associated with the consumption of vegetables (and fruit too!)

- Vital for health and maintenance of the human body

- Reduces the risk of many chronic diseases

- An important source of potassium, fiber, folic acid, vitamin a, vitamin d

- Reduces blood pressure due to potassium

- Reduces cholesterol due to dietary fiber

- Reduces the risk of fetal defects in pregnant women due to the folic acid content

- Improves immune system

- Improves skin and eyes due to vitamin a

- Numerous benefits associated with vitamin c including oral health, iron absorption, and healing

- Reduces the risk of heart disease and illness associated with it

- Studies have shown that vegetables can combat specific cancers

- Healthy diets combat obesity and diabetes

- Combats Osteoporosis and some renal issues

  - When eating more vegetables (and/or fruits) their high water levels aid in making you get the full feeling faster, and thus, help those that are trying to lose weight. It is low in calories, in conjunction with this, helps us to stay well below the daily required caloric intake.

Whatever you choose to grow, always keep in mind the harmony of the ecosystem, the rate, and extent to which your fish or plants will grow. As mentioned earlier in this chapter, temperature and location are also very important factors in your selection process. It is vital to the success of the Aquaponics garden, that you take the time to learn about the fish and plants for your developing ecosystem.

Some important things you should consider when selecting your plants and fish:

Let's start with plants:

First, in considering which plants to purchase, especially if they are going to be used specifically for consumption, it is important to note that because you are utilizing water-based methods versus soil-based methods, your production rate at its bare minimum will be 20-25% higher. Therefore, due to the fact that you are yielding such high quantities, determine which vegetation you will use for farming and which vegetation you would be willing to incorporate preservation methods such as canning or dehydrating, like some like to do with herbs and fruit.

Second, the suitable range for most vegetables is 18 to 30 degrees Celsius which converts to a temperature range of 64.4 to 89.6 degrees Fahrenheit. Winter vegetables do best in temperature ranges of 8 to 20 degrees Celsius (46.4 to 68 degrees Fahrenheit). Summer vegetables will do best in temperature ranges between 17 to 30 degrees Celsius (62.6 to 86 degrees Fahrenheit). Within these ranges, different vegetables and plants have different requirements, though they may do fine within the range assigned to their seasonal type, the specific required range will yield the best results. Leafy greens, for example, fall in the winter vegetable category, however, they prefer even cooler temperatures than most, requiring temperature ranges between 14 to 20 degrees Celsius (57.2 to 68 degrees Fahrenheit), mostly after sundown. Following the winter vegetable guidelines of range, if they were exposed to increased temperatures near the higher portion of the range, the flavor of these vegetables would be negatively impacted and inedible to most. More important than air temperature is water temperature, which has a far greater effect on the plants, however, both are equally important to monitor.

Third, when growing flowering plants or plants that yield fruit, light is an important factor. Each requires different amounts of daylight and/or darkness to cause the flowering or fruiting process to occur. Medicinal plants and some peppers fall into the category of short-day plants. This means they need more darkness and others such as many ornamentals fall into the category of long day plants because they require much more light than others to yield their beautiful blooms. All plants generally come with care guidelines when you purchase them but it is important in your planning process to do this research ahead of time to ensure that you are prepared and have an action plan for your production goals. There are plants, like most vegetables, that are light neutral, which makes things a bit easier to maintain and control.

Fourth, I have listed quite a few plants used in Aquaponics but the list of plant growth success with herbs, small trees, vegetables, and flowers is up around 150 and growing. Knowing the needs of your plants and matching those needs to your fish properly will help you to expand your selection of plants and the success you have in Aquaponics. In saying this, always remember, the goal is to keep everyone healthy and fed—people, fish, and plants—so, to achieve this goal, we must understand nutrient requirements. Different species have different nutrient requirements—some need more, some need less. For example, if you are planning on growing fruiting vegetable plants like tomatoes, peppers, cucumbers, eggplants, avocados, or fruits like strawberries and winter melon, they require higher nutrient-rich diets so they are better matched with a well established Aquaponics system in which the fish are able to yield the amounts of nutrients they need. Additionally, amongst these various species are root crops. These plants are better suited for a system in which deep media beds are utilized and they are very high maintenance so it may not be a good choice for you to attempt in an Aquaponics system. Leafy greens, legumes, and herbs are the most popular choices for Aquaponics because they have a low nutrient requirement. In the center of the nutrient, demand spectrum would be things like cabbage, cauliflower or broccoli. Radish falls on the very low end of the spectrum while beets, onions, and carrots fall somewhere between the center of the spectrum and the higher side of the demand spectrum.

Fifth, some plants grow much larger than others. This is the case with fruiting plants. If space is an issue, keep this in mind when selecting your plants. Also, depending on the type of system set up you choose, this could influence greatly which plants you will be able to grow. For example, bulbous or root based plants are better suited for media based beds versus a nutrient film technique system or a deep water culture system due to the support system and growing environment needed for these plants to flourish.

Lastly, because of the variations in needs of the different plants, and likewise the varying needs of the fish needed to coexist with these plants for a balanced ecosystem, it is important to ensure balance in all areas to maintain balance overall! Mixing plants with different nutrient needs or harvesting timeframes, for example, could result in great imbalance for all of the creatures in the ecosystem as an attempt to compensate for differing needs. Any unbalance that cannot be easily corrected can cause the entire ecosystem to fail.

Notes: If you are planting something that requires a long term grow period, it would be a good idea to plant some short term grow period plants with them. This way you not only reap the benefit of farm to table on a regular basis but the plants work together. For example, eggplants take a long time to mature so adding in herbs, tomatoes, and leafy greens around them yields quickly for your main salad ingredients, and will offer shading to the eggplant that it needs while also working with the other plants to clean the water for the fish. This maintains a balanced nutrient level, thus creating a healthy environment. Smart planning in your planting design can not only be beneficial in maximizing space but it can also aid in attracting beneficial insects and greatly improve your plant production.

Obviously, there is a lot to consider when selecting your plants, whether you want them for food consumption or simply want a houseplant or flowering plant. Always keep in mind the harmony of all species in your ecosystem, when making your decisions.

Obviously, the fish and the plants need to be a match made in heaven but the other important thing here, especially when it comes to foods we plan on consuming, is what you personally enjoy. I mean, let's be honest here, what is the point of all this work (except maybe satisfaction of achievement) if you aren't able to enjoy what you have produced? Why grow tomatoes if you don't plan on eating them? Why grow a flower you have allergies too? You wouldn't obviously.

That being said, if you know that you eat certain vegetables very often such as the common salad ingredients or herbs that you need for seasoning your foods, you would be more inclined to select these options to grow and the amount that you grow would be higher than say an artichoke, which you may eat when you are in the mood for it. There is no rule of thumb here. Everyone has different tastes so I will not tell you what to put in the garden but simply offer knowledge about the different options and things to consider.

To support this sentiment, I have put together some information that should prove useful in your Aquaponics vegetable planning below, but first I want to address the non-edible variety of plants. Edible varieties of plants are not the only plants well suited for Aquaponics, in fact, some of the best options for Aquaponics gardening are ornamental varieties of plants and Aquaponics is exceptionally successful in growing many kinds of houseplants. Roses are one of the most popular and successful of flowering plants, though there are many others that you can grow. House plants are a great way to keep the air clean and the house looking beautiful. Many varieties thrive in Aquaponics such as ferns and philodendrons, to name just two. You can pretty much grow just about anything from vegetables to plants to flowers, with proper environment set up, except blueberries and azaleas (due to their high acid needs) and of course the root crops like potatoes are really difficult to grow because of their need for a deep media bed, but even these, like carrots, for instance, have been grown successfully. The most effective and proven process for planting root based vegetables is that these should be planted in wicking beds which are attached to the media beds.

Ornamental plants have seen great success in Aquaponics gardens due to the constant flow of water and nutrients it receives. In addition to the roses, some great outdoor options are asters, lilies, daisies, forget-me-nots, hollies, and lavender.

Here is a list of some of the best options for indoor plants with information on whether you can use seeds or cuttings for best results:

• Spider Plants can be grown from either a seed or from cuttings.

• Female Dragon can be grown from either a seed or from cuttings.

• Chinese Money Plants can be grown from either a seed or from cuttings.

• Philodendrons can be grown from either a seed or from cuttings.

• Peace Lilies can be grown from seeds or from cuttings.

• Chinese evergreen can be grown from either a seed or from a cutting but it is suggested that you start with cutting because growing these from seeds is very difficult in Aquaponics systems.

• Devil's Ivy cannot be grown from seed but can be grown from cutting. Leopard Lilies, also known as Dumb Cane, cannot be grown from seeds but can be grown from cuttings. Arrowhead Vines cannot be grown from seeds but can be grown from cuttings.

The smell and taste of fresh herbs is absolutely amazing. My mouth is watering just thinking about it. Lucky for us, herbs are one of the easiest things to grow in an Aquaponics garden. Tarragon, Peppermint, Green Mint, Oregano, Basil, Sage, Stevia, Lemon Balm, Rosemary, and Cilantro are just some of the herbs you can grow and yes, you can grow from both seeds and cuttings, with the exception of Tarragon and Peppermint, but I strongly suggest always using cuttings because it gets your plants to grow stronger and faster.

Lettuce, spinach, bok choy, tomatoes, peppers, cucumbers, and celery are some of the most popular Aquaponics choices and all can be grown from either seeds or cuttings, however, as I said earlier, I am going to go into further detail on vegetables and expand past this list so that you can have more information to help you make decisions when planning your garden selections:

Let's start with the leafy greens because they are the basis to almost any salad and there are so many varieties to choose from. This, of course, is why it is number one on the Aquaponics selection list. It grows fast and it is easy to maintain. Aside from this, instead of having to harvest the entire head of lettuce, leaving the unused portion in your refrigerator with the potential to wilt, you can simply go to your garden and pull the leaves off that you need at that moment.

You not only get a freshly picked salad ingredient, but you allow the lettuce to continue to grow and remain healthy. So many perks to Aquaponics, trust me you will be hooked too. The leafy varieties are preferred over iceberg for two reasons other than taste preference. One, they pack more nutrients in them for our health and two, because they grow in only 30 days, whereas Iceberg takes 90 days. Remember what I said about making everyone happy in your ecosystem harmony? Well, we can't talk about our vegetables without at least giving a brief mention to our fish (I will get into them in greater detail later in this chapter). The majority of leafy green varieties prefer air temperature ranges between 60 and 80 degrees Fahrenheit.

This is just the exposed part of our favorite lettuce. We cannot forget about the needs of the root system which is exposed to the water. As I said before, though both are important, the water is even more important and leafy greens prefer their water to be in the temperature range of 70 to 74 degrees Fahrenheit. (Here is where our fish friends get their brief mention) Tilapia happens to be one of the fish that is a perfect match for our lettuce to thrive because they too prefer their water to be in the temperature ranges of 70 to 74 degrees Fahrenheit. This covers all your leafy greens like spinach, watercress, and arugula as well as all your herbs such as chives, basil, and rosemary.

Let's break this down further:

- LETTUCE (MIXED SALAD LEAVES)

- pH level ranges are 6.0 to 7.0

- Plant spacing requirements are 18 to 30 cm (20 to 25 heads/m²)

- Germination time and temperature will be 3 to 7 days at 13to 21 degrees Celsius

- Growth time is about 30 days (longer for some varieties like Iceberg)

- Temperature range is 15 to 22 degrees Celsius (flowering over 24 degrees Celsius)

- Light exposure needed is full sun

- Plant height is 20 to 30 cm tall and plant width is 25 to 35 cm wide

- Recommended Aquaponic method can be either media bed, NFT or DWC

The lettuce grows really well in an Aquaponics environment when nutrient concentrations in the water are more than sufficient. A number of them can be grown such as crisphead lettuce (iceberg), which has crispy leaves and a tight head, and is ideally suited for cool temps; butterhead lettuce has leaves that are loosely layered on another and tastes a bit sweet with no bitterness; Romaine lettuce has upright and tightly layered dark green leaves that are slow to seed and are sweet in taste; and loose leaf lettuce comes in a variety of colors and shapes with no head and can be directly planted on media beds and harvested by picking single leaves without collecting the whole plant.

This allows for the plant to continue growth and for the grower to avoid having unused, harvested lettuce wilt. Lettuce is a winter vegetable, so it requires night temperatures to range between 3 and 12 degrees Celsius for head growth, and day temperatures to range between 17 and 28 degrees Celsius. Lettuce is highly dependent on light and temperature for proper growth conditions. It requires extended daylight and warm conditions that are more than 18 degrees Celsius at night can cause seeding. Water temperatures more than 26 degrees Celsius may also cause seeding and bitter leaves. Lettuce does not have a high nutrient demand, but it is advised that you increase calcium concentrations in your water in order to prevent the tips of the leaves from burning during summer months.

The preferred pH is 5.8 to 6.2, but lettuce will still grow well with a pH level as high as 7, however, the lettuce could suffer from iron deficiencies at the higher pH levels. I would suggest that seedlings be transplanted to your Aquaponic set up around the three-week mark or when they are showing about 2 to 3 leaves. Adding phosphorus to the seedlings in the second and third weeks will aid in favorable root growth and help you to avoid stressing the plant when it is transplanted. Seedlings have an improved survival rate if they are exposed to colder temperatures direct sunlight for approximately 3 to 5 days prior to transplantation. On the contrary, when replanting in warm weather, light shade should be placed over the plants for two to three days beforehand to avoid water stress. If you maintain high nitrate levels, you should see faster growth rates as well as crisp, sweeter lettuce results.

- SWISS CHARD, also known as MANGOLD

- pH levels are 6 to 7.5

- Plant spacing requirements are 30 to 30 cm (15 to 20 plants/m²)

- Germination time and temperature will be 3 to 7 days at 25 to 30 degrees Celsius

- Growth time is about 25 to 35 days

- Temperature range is 16 to 24 degrees Celsius

- Light exposure needed is full sun (partial shade for temperatures greater than 26 degrees Celsius)

- Plant height and width will be 30 to 60 cm tall and 30 to 40 cm wide

- Recommended Aquaponic method can be either media beds, NFT pipes or DWC

It is a very popular leafy green vegetable to grow using Aquaponics, because it does not require high levels of nitrate and requires very little potassium and phosphorous, it is ideally suited for Aquaponics growth. Swiss chard has a fast growth rate and high nutritional value.

Though it is known as a leafy "green", it has amazing hints of yellow, purple and/ or red throughout its stem. Swiss chard is generally a late winter to spring vegetable however it prefers temperatures ranging between 16 and 24 degrees Celsius. Since it is a cool weather vegetable, it has the ability to survive temperatures as low as 5 degrees Celsius, yet it has also been known to fare well during mild summers. Swiss chard actually has a reasonable acceptance of salinity, which makes it an ideal plant for salt water. (This means it would be a great match for your Barramundi fish.) Swiss Chard is one of those leafy greens that allows us to remove larger leaves for use and leave the plant behind for the continued growth of new leaves.

Herbs: (We will highlight Basil and Parsley, to use for your guidelines to herbs)

- BASIL

- pH levels are 5.5 to 6.5

- Plant spacing requirements are 15 to 25 cm (8 to 40 plants/m²)

- Germination time and temperatures are 6 to 7 days with temperatures at 20 to 25 degrees Celsius

- Growth time is about 5 to 6 weeks (harvest begins when the plant is about 15 cm)

- Temperature ranges are 18 to 30 degrees Celsius but are best at 20 to 25 degrees Celsius

- Light exposure needed is Sunny or lightly shaded

- Plant height and width will be 30 to 70 cm tall and 30 cm wide

- Recommended Aquaponic method can be either media beds, NFT or DWC uptake, however, it is important to avoid too much nutrient depletion in the water.

Basil seeds need a very high and constant temperature in order for germination to begin (20 to 25 degrees Celsius). After they have been transplanted to the media bed or desired set up, the basil will grow best in warm to very warm conditions and lots of sun with minimal shading for optimal leaves. If temperatures throughout the day exceed 27 degrees Celsius, the plants will need to be in a ventilated and or shaded area to prevent the tips of the leaves from burning. It is best to transplant new seedlings once they have 4 or 5 leaves. To avoid disease, stress, or mold, air ventilation is vital and water temperatures should be maintained above 21 degrees Celsius at all times. Once the plant is about 15 cm tall, you can harvest the leaves and continue to do so for 30 to 50 days. Make sure to leave a few flowering plants behind because they will attract beneficial insects that can improve the entire garden and help to keep a constant supply of basil seeds in production.

- PARSLEY

- pH levels are 6 to 7

- Plant spacing requirements are 15 to 30 cm (10 to 15 plants/m²)

- Germination time and temperature ranges are 8 to 10 days and 20 to 25 degrees Celsius

- Growth time will be about 20 to 30 days after transplantation

- Temperatures are 15 to 25 degrees Celsius

- Light exposure is full sun and partial shade when greater than 25 degrees Celsius

- Plant height and width are 30 to 60 cm tall and 30 to 40 cm wide

- Recommended aquaponic method can be either media beds, NFT or DWC

Parsley is a very common herb to grow due to its high levels of vitamins A and C, calcium and iron). Parsley is an easy herb to grow and has a low nutrient requirement. Parsley is a biennial herb, but it is traditionally grown as an annual. Highly resistant to temperatures as low as zero degrees Celsius but should not be exposed to temperatures lower than 8 degrees Celsius for optimal growth. Parsley needs full sunlight for up to eight hours a day.

It should have partial shading if temperatures are greater than 25 degrees Celsius. Initial germination can take 2 to 5 weeks, depending on seeds freshness.

Emerging seedlings will have the appearance of grass, with two narrow seed leaves opposite each other. After approximately 5 to 6 weeks you will be able to transplant the seedlings into your aquaponic setup. You can begin to harvest once the individual stalks of Parsley are at least 15 cm. If you harvest from the outside in, you will encourage growth production throughout the season. Many people remove the tops, but this will simply slow production.

Next, we will discuss tomatoes. Tomatoes have a complicated growth cycle and go through many changes during this time. There are two types of tomato plants amongst the variety of tomatoes.

One type yields tomatoes all at one time and the other will yield tomato production periodically and continuously. This is important because if you choose the one that yields all at once, this species is a much smaller plant that doesn't need a support structure and can easily be grown indoors. The other species will vary in size dependent on the variety. Tomato plants require high humidity and prefer a temperature of 78 degrees Fahrenheit in order to yield fruit. Though this is their preference, tomatoes can yield fruit in temperatures ranging from 68 to 88 degrees Fahrenheit. It is important to maintain pH levels between 5.8 and 6.8 but can handle pH levels up 7.2. They require up to 12 hours of light per day and no less than 8 hours per day.

The more light they get, the more fruit they will yield and the faster the plant will yield it. It is best to start from a cutting. If you start from seeds, you must have a separate seedling tray with a temperature at 77 degrees Fahrenheit and humidity at 100 percent. They will need to grow 2 to 6 weeks before transplanting them to the grow bed.

- TOMATO

- pH levels are 5.5 to 6.5

- Plant spacing requirements are 40 to 60 cm (3 to 5 plants/m²)

- Germination time and temperature are: 4 to 6 days in 20 to 30 degrees Celsius

- Growth time will be 50 to 70 days till first harvest and fruiting 90 to 120 days upwards of 8 to 10 months (dependent on variety)

- Optimal temperatures are 13 to 16 degrees Celsius at night, 22 to 26 degrees Celsius during daytime

- Light exposure is full sun

- Plant height and width will be 60 to 180 cm tall and 60 to 80 cm wide

- Recommended Aquaponic method can be either media beds or DWC

Tomatoes are an excellent summer fruiting vegetable but they require structural support systems. It is important to consider the plant to fish ratios due to the high nutrient requirement of tomatoes. For proper growth, a high nitrogen concentration is needed during the early stages and potassium is needed during the flowering stage as well.

Tomatoes enjoy warm temperatures with full sun exposure. If temperatures drop below 8 to 10 degrees Celsius, the plants will cease growth. Likewise, anything above 40 degrees Celsius can cause flowers to stop growing and the fruit to turn. Tomatoes have a moderate tolerance to salinity, which makes them suitable for areas where pure freshwater is not available. Higher saline levels during the fruiting stage can improve the quality of the tomato.

Set stakes or plant support structures before transplanting to prevent root damage. You can transplant the seedlings at the 3 to 6-week mark, when the seedling is about 10 to 15 cm and when nighttime temperatures are consistently above 10 degrees Celsius.

Once the plants reach a height of 60 cm, you need to determine whether you will continue the growth process as a bush or single stem, and you do so by pruning the unnecessary upper branches. Remove the leaves from the bottom 30 cm of the main stem for better air circulation and reduction of potential disease. Remove the leaves that are covering each fruit branch prior to ripening to aid in the proper flow of nutrition to the fruits and to accelerate growth.

Vegetables like cabbage, broccoli, cauliflower, radishes and kale all have similar preferences in the environment.

- Cauliflower

- pH levels are 6.0 to 6.5

- Plant spacing requirements are 45 to 60 cm (3 to 5 plants/m²)

- Germination time and temperature are 4 to 7 days with temperature 8 to 20 degrees Celsius

- Growth time is 2 to 3 months during spring and 3 to 4 months during autumn

- Temperatures are 20 to 25 degrees Celsius for initial growth and 10 to 15 degrees Celsius for head setting in autumn

- Light exposure is full sun

- Plant height and width is 40 to 60 cm tall and 60 to 70 cm wide

- Recommended Aquaponic method is media beds.

Cauliflower requires calcium for the production of heads. It is a very climate sensitive plant, therefore, selecting a suitable variety for your environment and ensuring proper timing for transplant is paramount for this plant to flourish.

Preferred air temperature for the initial growth period of the plant is 15 to 25 degrees Celsius. Head formation requires colder temperatures of 10 to 15 degrees Celsius in autumn or 15 to 20 degrees Celsius in spring, as long as there is a good amount of humidity and full sun conditions. Cold temperatures are tolerated but there is a danger of frost damage. Also, light shade is good in warmer temperatures greater than 23 degrees Celsius.

When plants are 3 to 5 weeks old and have 4 to 5 leaves, you can begin transplantation. Make sure they are placed about 50 cm apart.

To keep the heads white, use string or rubber bands to keep the leaves covering it. When they reach about 6 to 10 cm in diameter, the harvest may take less than a week in ideal temperatures or as long as a month in cooler conditions. Harvest when the heads are compact, white and firm. Cauliflower is susceptible to pests, so it is important to incorporate some sort of pest control.

- Head Cabbage

- pH level is 6 to 7.2

- Plant spacing requirements are 60 to 80 cm (4 to 8 plants/m²)

- Germination time and the temperature is 4 to 7 days with 8 to 29 degrees Celsius

- Growth time will be 45 to 70 days from transplanting (dependent on variety and climate)

- The preferred temperature is 15 to 20 degrees Celsius (growth ceases greater than 25 degrees Celsius)

- Light exposure is full sun

- Plant height and width is 30 to 60 cm high and 30 to 60 cm wide

- Recommended Aquaponic method is media beds

Cabbage is a winter crop with preferred growing temperatures of about 15 to 20 degrees Celsius.

It is important to harvest the cabbage prior to daytime temperatures reaching 23 to 25 degrees Celsius. When the heads begin to grow, it is vital that they have high concentrations of phosphorus and potassium. You will want to transplant seedlings when there are about 4 to 6 leaves and are at a height of 15 cm.

Start harvesting when cabbage heads are firm and about 10 to 15 cm in diameter depending on the variety grown.

- Broccoli

  - pH levels are 6 to 7

  - Plant spacing requirements are 40 to 70 cm (3 to 5 plants/m²)

  - Germination time and the temperature is 4 to 6 days with 25 degrees Celsius

  - Growth time will be 60 to 100 days from transplantation

  - Average daily temperature preferred is 13 to 18 degrees Celsius

  - Light exposure is full sun. It can tolerate partial shade but will mature slowly.

  - Plant height and width is 30 to 60 cm tall and 30 to 60 cm wide

  - Recommended Aquaponic method is media beds

Broccoli growth is optimal when daytime temperatures are 14 to 17 degrees Celsius. Winter varieties require temperatures of 10 to 15 degrees Celsius for head formation.

Broccoli can withstand higher temperatures if a higher humidity is present. Hot temperatures cause premature seeding. You can transplant seedlings into media beds once 4 to 5 leaves are visible and the plants are 15 to 20 cm tall. Seedlings need to be placed 40 to 50 cm apart. Broccoli is susceptible to pests so it is very important to maintain pest control methods. You can begin harvesting broccoli when the buds of the head are firm and tight.

Cucumbers, squash, and melons are vine crops and they have pretty much the same requirements for growth. These types of vegetables prefer temperatures ranging from 75 to 78 degrees Fahrenheit during the day and around 68 degrees Fahrenheit at night. Humidity levels must be no greater than 75 percent. They can take anywhere from 1 ½ to 2 months for full growth from seeds. There are many squash varieties such as summer squash like zucchini and yellow squash and the numerous winter squash like butternut, spaghetti, and acorn.

Assorted melons include watermelon, cantaloupe, and honeydew.

- Cucumbers

- pH levels are 5.5 to 6.5

- Plant spacing requirements are 30 to 60 cm (depending on variety; 2 to 5 plants/m²)

- Germination time and the temperature is 3 to7 days with 20 to 30 degrees Celsius

- Growth time is 55 to 65 days

- Temperature is 22 to 28 degrees Celsius during the daytime, 18 to 20 degrees Celsius nightly; highly susceptible to frost.

- Light exposure is full sun

- Plant height and width is 20 to 200 cm tall and 20 to 80 cm wide

- Recommended Aquaponic methods are media beds and DWC

Cucumbers, as well as squash, zucchini, and melons, are great summer vegetables. They are ideally suited to grow in media beds because they have a large root structure.

Cucumbers can also be grown on floating rafts, but if you choose this method it is important to constantly check to grow pipes because there could be the risk of clogging from excessive root growth.

Cucumbers require large quantities of nitrogen and potassium, so it is important to ensure proper plant to fish ratios. Cucumbers grow best with high humidity, lots of sunshine, and warm nights. They enjoy growth temperatures of 24 to 27 degrees Celsius during the daytime with 70 to 90 percent humidity. Plants cease growth and production at 10 to 13 degrees Celsius. Higher potassium concentration is preferred for higher fruit settings and yields. Cucumber seedlings can be transplanted at 2 to 3 weeks when there are 4 to 5 leaves showing.

They grow very quickly. For optimal health of the fruit, you should cut their apical tips when the stem is two meters long, allowing more nutrient flow to the fruit. Remove the lateral branches to allow for enhanced ventilation. It is important to have beneficial insects around your cucumbers. It is also important to provide a support system for their growth and prevention of diseases and/ or molds. Once transplanted, cucumbers can start production in about 2 to 3 weeks. The plants can be harvested in ideal conditions 10 to 15 times. Make sure to harvest every few days to prevent the fruits from excessive growth and to promote new growth.

- Eggplant

- pH level is 5.5 to 7.0

- Plant spacing requirements are 40 to 60 cm (3 to 5 plants/m²)

- Germination time and the temperature is 8 to 10 days with 25 to 30 degrees Celsius

- Growth time will be 90 to 120 days

- Temperatures preferred are 15 to 18 degrees Celsius at night and 22 to 26 degrees Celsius during the day; highly susceptible to frost

- Light exposure is full sun

- Plant height and width is 60 to 120 cm tall and 60 to 80 cm wide

- Recommended Aquaponic method is media beds

Eggplant is a summer fruiting vegetable that grows well in media beds because of their deep root system growth. These plants can produce 10 to 15 fruits for a total yield of 3 to 7 kg. Eggplants have high nitrogen and potassium requirements.

Because of this, it is important to ensure a proper balance throughout the ecosystem. Eggplants enjoy warm temperatures with full exposure to sunlight. They grow best with daily temperatures in the range of 22 to 26 degrees Celsius and humidity of 60 to 70 percent. Temperatures less than 9 to 10 degrees Celsius and more than 30 to 32 degrees Celsius can cause growth and production cessation. Seeds germinate in 8 to 10 days in warm temperatures ranging between 26 to 30 degrees Celsius.

Seedlings can be transplanted when 4 to 5 leaves are showing. Near the end of the summer, start pinching off new blooms to promote the ripening of any existing fruit. Towards the end of the season, plants can be pruned at 20–30 cm, leaving just three branches for the following season. This will stop any further growth until favorable seasons return. Start harvesting when the eggplants are 10–15 cm long. The skin should be shiny and deep purple.

- Beans And Peas

- pH level is 5.5 to 7.0

- Plant spacing requirements are 10 to 30 cm dependent on variety (bush varieties 20 to40 plants/m², climbing varieties 10 to 12 plants/m²)

- Germination time and the temperature is 8 to 10 days with 21 to 26 degrees Celsius

- Growth time is 50 to 110 days to reach maturity depending on the variety

- Temperature is 16 to 18 degrees Celsius nightly, 22 to 26 degrees Celsius daytime

- Light exposure is full sun

- Plant height and width is 60 to 250 cm (climbing) and 60 to 80 cm (bush)

- Recommended Aquaponic method is media bed

Beans have low nitrate needs but have a moderate demand in terms of phosphorus and potassium. Beans are recommended for newly established units as they may fix atmospheric nitrogen for you.

Climbing varieties prefer full sunlight but will tolerate partial shade in warm conditions. Bean plants do not grow in temperatures lower than 12 to 14 degrees Celsius. Temperatures greater than 35 degrees Celsius can cause flower and fruit growth cessation. They enjoy humidity of 70 to 80 percent. It is important to choose the right varieties according to the location and season.

In general, climbing varieties are cultivated in summer while others are better suited for spring and autumn conditions. Beans are susceptible to aphids and spider mites. It is a good idea to employ regular pest control procedures and attention needs to be paid as to which companion plants are placed in the garden in an effort to avoid cross-contamination in case any treatment has to be carried out. Snap bean varieties such as green or yellow wax beans have pods that need to be firm and crisp at harvest.

Try to avoid pulling off branches that can offer future pods when pulling off the pods you are harvesting currently. Make sure to pick all pods off in order to keep plants productive. Shell beans such as black, broad or fava beans should be picked when the pods change color and the beans inside are fully formed but not dried out. Pods should be plump and firm.

Dried beans such as kidney beans and soybeans need to become as dry as possible before cooler weather sets in or when plants have turned brown and lost most of their leaves. These pods will easily open when very dry, making seed removal a simple procedure.

- Peppers

- pH level is 5.5 to 6.5

- Plant spacing requirements are 30 to 60 cm (3 to 4 plants/m 2, or more for small-sized plant varieties)

- Germination time and the temperature is 8 to 12 days with 22 to 30 degrees Celsius (seeds will not germinate at a temperature lower than 13 degrees Celsius)

- Growth time is 60 to 95 days

- Temperature is 14 to 16 degrees Celsius at night time, 22 to 30 degrees Celsius during the daytime

- Light exposure is full sun

- Plant height and width is 30 to 90 cm tall and 30 to 80 cm wide

- Recommended Aquaponics method is media beds

There are numerous varieties of peppers with numerous assortments of color and varying degrees of Scoville levels (heat index). Regardless whether they are sweet bell pepper, hot chili peppers (jalapeño or cayenne peppers), or anything in between, they can all be grown in your Aquaponics garden.

Peppers are best grown with the media bed system though they can also grow in 11 cm diameter NFT pipes if they have a good structural support system. Peppers are a summer fruiting vegetable that prefers warm conditions and full exposure to sunlight. Seeds germinate in temperatures at about 22 to 34 degrees Celsius.

They cannot germinate well in temperatures below 15 degrees Celsius. Best conditions for fruiting are daytime temperatures of 22 to 28 degrees Celsius and night-time temperatures of 14 to 16 degrees Celsius. They also enjoy humidity of 60 to 65 percent. The best temperatures for the root levels are 15 to 20 degrees Celsius. Air temperatures below 10 to 12 degrees Celsius will cause plant growth cessation and additionally cause abnormally formed fruits.

Temperatures that are higher than 30 to 35 degrees Celsius can lead to problems with the flowers and even cause them to fall off. Basically, peppers that are spicier can be grown at higher temperatures. The top leaves of the plant protect the fruit that is hanging below from getting sun exposure. As with other fruiting plants, nitrate is vital for the initial growth process.

The best range of nitrate levels needed is 20–120 mg/liter but higher concentrations of potassium and phosphorus are needed for flowering and fruiting. Seeds should be transplanted when the plant shows 6 to 8 leaves and the night temperatures remain constant above 10 degrees Celsius. A strong structural support system is needed for bushy, heavy-yielding plants. Stakes or vertical strings hanging from iron wires pulled horizontally above the units should anchor them properly.

If growing red sweet peppers, you need to leave the green fruits on the plants until they ripen and turn red. In order to encourage future plant growth, you should pick the first couple of flowers that make their appearance on the plant. Should excessive fruit setting occur, you will need to reduce the number of flowers on the plant.

This will aid in promoting the growth of fruit to adequate sizes. You should begin harvesting when peppers reach appropriate sizes.

Peppers need to be left on the plants until they ripen fully. You will recognize this by the change in color. Harvesting them at their optimal ripeness will improve their levels of vitamin C. If you harvest regularly throughout the season, your plants will continue to blossom fruit and promote growth. Peppers can be easily stored fresh for 10 days at 10 degrees Celsius with 90 to 95 percent humidity or they can be dehydrated or pickled for long-term storage.

Ornamental fish for Aquaponics Fish Tanks:

Some people simply want to reap the benefits of the Aquaponics system for Vegan consumption and enjoy the beauty of the fish that aid in the growth of their vegetables and herbs. Others too, want a purely ornamental set up for their home and are not concerned with food production at all. In either case, there are many fish to choose from.

It is important to keep in mind the needs of the ecosystem as a whole to determine the size of the fish and/ or the amount of fish that you need in order to maintain proper balance throughout. Here are some suggestions for ornamental fish for the indoor tank:

- Angelfish are also known as the Koi Angel and come in many types and colors. Generally, they will be approximately six inches in size, therefore, a 20-gallon tank would be the minimum suggested and of course, is dependent on the amount of fish you desire.
- Goldfish tends to be the staple for home aquariums. These fish also come in many varieties differing in color, size, and shape. They are very durable fish so they can handle any size tank and do not require heat. They pretty much eat anything as they are not very picky eaters so the variety of foods and plants to choose from for their consumption are countless. Goldfish produce a large amount of waste for such a small fish, which actually makes them great for Aquaponics garden to grow. Because they tend to be shy, it is important to have plants in the tank itself for some type of retreat for the fish. The ideal water temperatures for Goldfish would be between 68 and 75 degrees Fahrenheit.
- Bloodfin Tetras are also very hardy fish that can withstand almost any environment. They are very beautiful with silver and red hues and therefore make for an attractive setup.
- The White Cloud Mountain Minnow is a small pretty fish well suited for the indoor aquarium as well as the outdoor pond! They do well with cold water conditions.
- Danios are also a small fish that are very durable fish that do well in almost any environment. They have beautiful striped features and bright colors that look amazing as they race around your tank, traveling in schools. These fish will

come to greet you at the top of the water when you feed them their flakes so you may enjoy a setup that has the plants placed on one side while the water is exposed for feeding on the other.

Note: In colder areas, heaters may be warranted to ensure that the water does not get too cold. The same would be the case for extremely hot areas where the temperatures can reach into the three digits. It is important to maintain regular temperature ranges and not have the fish experience drastic fluctuations to stress them out, no matter how durable the species may be. Temperatures should never fluctuate more than three degrees!

For those of you who would like to enjoy outdoor ponds using Aquaponics, Koi are no doubt the most popular choice. These fish are not just beautiful and come in assorted colors, but they are omnivorous, parasite-resistant and thus live very long life spans upwards of 60 years.

They produce an abundant amount of waste so they are great at helping the plants in and around your pond grow large and fast. One thing to keep in mind about Koi, they are easy to find for purchasing however they are very expensive fish to buy. Due to their durability, unbelievable beauty, and long life, the cost may very well be worth it! How many fish can you honestly say with certainty (in the ornamental category) will live a good amount of time or even survive when you make your purchase.

Aside from making my pond area bear proof where I live, I am fairly certain that my investment in Koi is a good one that I will enjoy for years to come! (They may very well be there for the next generation after me to enjoy!)

Obviously, there are many freshwater fish to choose from so I am just going to cover a select few that tend to be the top choices for Aquaponics. You can use this guide to deviate from this list as many fish are related in one way or another (like the Carp, Goldfish, and Koi, for example).

- Tilapia seems to be the number one choice amongst Aquaponics growers. This is understandable because Tilapia are easy to breed and are fast growing fish that are basically ready to be on your plate within 6 to 9 months. They are a warm water breed that enjoys temperature ranges between 72 and 86 degrees Fahrenheit. Aside from their ease of breeding and fast growth, they are delicious with a mild flavor that is used in many cuisines in various culinary styles. These fish are durable and can adapt to many less desirable environments though they, like everyone else, have their preference, and it is very important to maintain constant warm water temperatures if you want to keep your fish healthy, breeding, and growing at a consistent pace. These fish are omnivorous and can be placed in tanks with other species without concern of them eating the other fish. It is important to note that Tilapia breed rapidly (about every four to six weeks) so you must have a tank large enough to contain all the new schools.
- Trout is another option however it is important to recognize that they must be closely monitored due to their high Dissolved Oxygen levels and pH balance. Anything that throws their environment out of whack can be detrimental. They are cold water fish that enjoy

temperature ranges between 56 and 68 degrees Fahrenheit. Trout can be ready for eating in 12 to 16 months though it is a more delicate fish than the warm water Tilapia, Trout is a great source of protein and Omega fatty acids and it is a delicious fish option. In reference to the marriage in this ecosystem, the options for your plants are reduced because of the colder water requirements, therefore it is important if choosing this fish that you also choose plants that are very hardy and can withstand cooler water temperatures.

- Perch is a highly adaptable fish that comes in a variety of silver, yellow and jade. Because of their adaptability, they have been a good option for the beginner Aquaponics growers. They can handle cooler water temperatures but their ideal temperature range would be between 70 and 82 degrees Fahrenheit. Depending on which variety of Perch you choose, you can be eating your Perch as early as 9 months or in the case of the silver Perch, up to 16 months. Perch are carnivorous fish so you need to feed them smaller fish, bugs, and shrimp. This may be a more expensive diet for your fish but the taste of Perch is worth it for those who can afford the additional expense.

- Catfish have become very popular options for Aquaponics because they grow extremely fast allowing the breeder to enjoy the taste of this delectable fish in only 5 to 10 months. Catfish are sensitive to water temperature, water quality, and pH like the Trout, so there is a need to be diligent with maintaining a pristine environment. They require temperature ranges between 78 and 86 degrees Fahrenheit. Catfish are bottom dwellers that come in many sizes. This fish offers great flavor and are high in vitamin D, which most people tend to be deficient in. One thing to note about catfish is that they do not have scales, so it is important to skin the fish before you prepare it for consumption.

- Barramundi is a special option, in that this fish, unlike the others, can be kept in both freshwater systems and saltwater systems. (Pleases note: Saltwater is not recommended for Aquaponics simply because of the lack of plant options available for your system.) Barramundi must not be kept with small fish because they will get very aggressive and can injure or even eat the younger smaller fish. This is a white fish that is very flaky and tasty, thus the reason for its popularity. They grow rather quickly and can be on your plate within 12 months time. These fish do require perfect water conditions and therefore need to be monitored regularly. Dissolved Oxygen levels need to be regulated. That being said, they are great fish to watch in your tank and they have a high waste output for a thriving garden.

- Largemouth, smallmouth, and striped Bass are very popular Aquaponics fish as well. They prefer a temperature range between 75 and 85 degrees Fahrenheit. Dependent on the type you choose, it will be fully matured for serving in 12 to 18 months, with Striped Bass growing quicker. They require pristine water conditions, dark areas (they do not like bright lights), they need proper oxygen and pH levels and must follow a strict feeding schedule. Bass is a very delicious source of food and like Tilapia, has been used in many culinary forms and cuisines, so the recipes are numerous.

- It's funny but most people don't think about Crustaceans when deciding to do Aquaponics, however they are gaining in popularity the more Aquaponics becomes known around the world. Thinking outside the "fish" box (or tank, I should say, lol), Crustaceans offer great variety for your meals and are definitely a viable choice in Aquaponics systems. The best part is that many fish can cohabitate with your crustaceans! Setting the carnivores aside, you can place Mussels, Oysters, Crayfish, freshwater prawns, shrimp, crabs, and even lobster, in your tank. Aside from a food source for us humans, they are great at keeping the tank clean because they tend to eat dead organic plant matter. Many people tend to keep a separate tank for their crustaceans if they are planning on using them for human food as opposed to fish food. Even if your fish won't eat them, many may decide to attack them, and just like fish, we want to keep them healthy and stress-free. Mussels are a bit different than the others in this category because they can grow in the tank as well as in the grow beds! For your prawns, they prefer temperature ranges between 82 and 88 degrees Fahrenheit and can be served within 6 to 12 months. Your lobster prefers 71 to 76 degrees Fahrenheit and can be served in 24 months. The oysters enjoy temperatures of 75 to 79 degrees Fahrenheit and can be on your plate in 24 months.

Special Mention: The past few years, we hear about cannabis in the news either about the medical breakthroughs they are reporting in terms of benefits in the fight against cancer, Alzheimer's, PTSD, seizures and other ailments or about how state after state is approving the legalization of cannabis. With that being said, I thought I would briefly mention that Aquaponics is also an area in which Cannabis growth has seen great success. Since we are discussing plants, there may be a few of you interested in attempting this. Though it is not new to Hydroponics, it is newer to Aquaponics but there are plenty of articles online and books on this subject if you should be interested in doing so and they discuss legal allowances for different regions as well as proper set up conducive to growth for these particular plants.

Chapter 4: How To Create A Proper Aquaponics Environment

You now have a good idea of what you would like your Aquaponics garden to look like and where it will be located. You know what kind of plants you want in your garden and what kind of fish you would like in your tank. The next step is to choose the system you feel would work best for you and work on all of the factors that are required to ensure that your Aquaponics ecosystem will function properly and allow your plants and fish to thrive.

Types Of Systems

Sun Pond

The basic set up is reminiscent of that used by the Aztecs. It simply consists of the plants floating directly on the pond or tank water with its roots submerged in the water. The biggest issue with this design arises with the inability to stop fish from eating and damaging the plants.

Flood and Drain

This is the most common of the Aquaponics systems, due to its simplicity. An even ratio of fish tank volume to plant bed volume makes for an easy calculation. The system utilizes three components: the fish tank, the pump, and the grow bed. Water is pumped directly from the fish tank to the media bed. The media bed then drains back into the fish tank. It's the circle of life! This works best with a single bed area. Having two or more can lead to low water levels and stress on the fish.

Chop

The acronym CHOP stands for constant height, one pump. This system is like the flood and drain except that there is the addition of the sump pump in order to maintain the water levels at a consistent height. The pump is located in a separate sump tank. The water from the fish tank overflows into the grow beds. The grow beds then drain into the sump tank which then pumps the water back to the fish tank.

This system is less stressful on the fish because of the water level maintenance but does require a lot more space and can present difficulties with supply needs. The set up for this system requires that the sump tank area is lower than the grow bed area which also needs to be lower than the fish tank.

Chop 2

This system obviously is very much like the CHOP except the way that it is set up is very different. The CHOP has a more vertical relation to each part where the CHOP2 is horizontal in relation to where its life producing tanks are located. This system requires that the fish tank and the media beds sit level with each other with the only part sitting below them being the sump tank area.

The sump tank pumps water to the media beds and the fish tank. The grow beds utilize an auto siphon to receive their much-needed water and the fish tank utilizes a gravity feed overflow mechanism. With this system, you can have two or more grow bed areas feeding off of the one fish tank. Doing so would require a larger setup and stronger pumping mechanisms. Because the sump tank doubles its duty, clean and dirty water mixes and filtration is not efficient. Additional filtration would be recommended in order to reach an optimal ecosystem environment.

Automation

There are so many things that go on in our day to day lives. If we could make one part of it that much easier and not have to think about it constantly, why wouldn't you?

An Aquaponics system can be run seamlessly on an automated system. Our ancestors did not have this luxury and had to maintain a rigorous schedule to ensure that they fed the fish, the water quality was tested, the temperature was as it should be, the filter was clear of any solid waste obstructions, and pumping mechanisms were doing their job.

These days, everything can be done by machines and computers and can even be monitored on smart devices from remote locations far away from the Aquaponics site. Sensors that are computer monitored don't have to be astronomically priced as they come in a range of prices and capacities. They are made to alert you when something in your system is not quite right and depends on what the problem is, they can automatically correct the problem. Not everyone is up to this technology. It does require some programming/setting. I still need help using my I-phone. Thank God for my kids. It's amazing what they know about technology even before they are teenagers.

For me, more simple systems of automation like timers work just fine, especially when you are using a flood and drain system. A timer must be set up to control the system as they use settings to cause the flood and drain to occur. The time is usually set for every hour on the hour for 15 minutes in duration, in an effort to fill the media beds. During the remaining 45 minutes of the hour, the media beds are draining into the fish tank.

For others, an auto siphon, also known as a bell siphon, is preferred. This method remains active at all times because it works through the use of an overflow spout. Once the water level rises causing overflow, the siphon automatically opens and releases the water from the media beds into the fish tank. Once the media bed is drained, the siphon closes again and waits to refill. The process will continue automatically unless a solid is caught in the siphon, causing a blockage.

If you are still interested in some type of automation at a budget but want something a bit more sophisticated, you might want to look into APDuino. APDuino is a firmware that is specifically designed for both Aquaponic and Hydroponic systems and can be set through wi-fi or hard-wired. There are others out there, so it is recommended that you do your research to see what best meets your needs and your budget.

Even for those who have been enjoying the relaxation of owning an aquarium, automatic feeders have become popular, especially for those with an assortment of fish with differing feeding needs. This is a great option for Aquaponics.

Aside from monitoring and repairing, automated systems have been beneficial in mimicking day and night. Shading and venting can be incorporated to ensure that the system is temperature regulated. The shade will minimize the heat produced from the sun and the vent will cool the garden by releasing the hot air that has accumulated. This, of course, is not a necessity since it is not difficult to open and close curtains and windows, however, if you are not near your Aquaponics garden for long periods of time (most people spend more time at work then they do at home) then this luxury doesn't sound so ridiculous, does it? Finding the right location for your garden that will allow for a good balance, may help to avoid the added expenditure.

Automatic lighting is another feature to consider indoors or out. It is important to have sunlight, but we don't always have sunny days and of course, when we do, it doesn't stay as day must go and night must come. Lighting doesn't just affect how much "sunlight" a plant gets but also the temperature the garden experiences. We will discuss lighting and temperatures in more detail later on in the chapter.

Biofiltration

Biofilters are made to duplicate the processes naturally occurring in nature. Aquaponics incorporates biofilters to ensure that it mimics mother nature's work as closely as humanly possible. Aquaponics systems make sure that no waste occurs as everything is vitally important just as it is in nature. Saying that, recycle and reuse is not just something we say but something we must do.

Aquaponics does just that since the excreta from the fish is used as a source of food for the garden and, just like any natural ecosystem, one hand washes the other, so the plants will clean the water for the fish. In the next chapter, we will discuss in detail the nutrient cycle, but biofilters are a part of that necessary cycle. The medium which facilitates the nutrient cycle is called a biofilter.

Regular aquariums require extensive filtration systems to achieve a healthy environment but with planted aquariums like in Aquaponics, the plants act as a natural biofilter, so the filtration needed is much less extensive and more inexpensive. In fact, in using the flood and drain method with media beds, added filtration is not needed. The plants in the Aquaponic garden remove all the nitrites and nitrates that are harmful to fish but stimulate growth in plants. If fish to plant bed ratios are properly calculated, biofiltration can simply be done by the plants. For the most part, in Aquaponics, this is the case. Sometimes the plants need a bit of help so additional filtration can be incorporated. This may occur in a DWC configured grow bed, but it is not likely needed with media beds.

Tanks

Depending on the type of system you choose, you may not only need a tank for your fish but a tank for your sump pump as well. Some people will additionally purchase a tank to grow fingerlings until they are big enough to survive in a tank with adult fish who might like to make a meal out of them. Generally, I like to keep one or the other so one tank would suffice.

It is important to keep in mind that aquariums are made for fish. Aquaponics gardens are made for plants and fish, edible fish mostly, and for that reason, the two don't automatically go together. Aquariums are chemically treated and require filtration systems to ensure that the water is not toxic to the fish who inhabit it. The biofiltration of plants in such an environment without an additional filtration system will cause algae to build up. Algae are detrimental to both plants and fish because it sucks the oxygen from the water for their own needs.

Additionally, ornamental fish versus fish breeds used for consumption have different environmental needs. A well-lit aquarium setting for Guppies, Mollies, or other ornamental fish, even Koi in a pond, works great but fish like Tilapia and Bluegill tend to prefer darker areas with places to hide, especially when they feel danger looming (and that could simply be someone looking in the tank).

Purchasing a kit, as previously discussed. It will ensure that you have the proper set up for your plants and fish. If you choose the DO IT YOURSELF path and want an aquarium as part of your set up, the size must be considered to determine if biofiltration by the plants will be suitable or if an additional filtration system is needed. Aquariums are safe and watertight for marine inhabitants so if the worst thing you need to add to your DO IT YOURSELF project budget is a filtration system, it's worth it.

Other containment systems can be used like barrels, tanks, bathtubs, etc. but again, this would be covered extensively in a DO IT YOURSELF manual specific to Aquaponics. These alternate containment systems do require many more steps to ensure that there is no toxic residue and that the parts you choose for your system are food grade and/or drinking water safe. It is better to be safe than sorry, not just for the living organisms, plants, and fish in your Aquaponics ecosystem, but also for the people who intend to consume the plants and/or fish cultivated in the garden. So, therefore, DO IT YOURSELF people, when in doubt, don't use it, count it as out!!!

Grow Beds

The general depth for Aquaponics' grow beds is 12 inches as that is optimal for growth, biofiltration, and temperatures. If you intend to utilize Aquaponics systems for large plants and/or trees, then doubling the depth to 24 inches is advised. For most grow beds, 12 inches is perfect to allow room for the root system and its natural processes. Whether your garden utilizes media (which allows, at this depth, biofiltration, conversion of ammonia to nitrate, to occur) or is directly submerging the roots in water (having the roots this deep allows for stability in temperature), 12 inches in depth has proven to deliver conditions conducive to a flourishing Aquaponics ecosystem.

Types Of Grow Beds:

Media Based

The most commonly used grow beds are those that use items like rocks or gravel for biofiltration. Media based refers to anything that is used to give a support system to the plants since they don't have the soil to do that function.

Media can include:

- Rocks

- Gravel

- Sand

- Perlite

- Styrofoam

- Mineral wood

- Clay beads

Mostly commonly used media:

- Gravel

- Expanded Shale

- Clay beads

The ideal size of the medium should be ¾ inches in diameter to allow for proper drainage from plant bed to fish tank.

Previously discussed in this book, it is important to consider weight when setting up your Aquaponics garden because it is not only the fish tank that has considerable weight (example: a 100 gallon fish tank weighs about 1150 pounds when filled with water) but the grow beds have a great amount of weight also, especially in those using media based beds.

The use of media in your beds allows for a broader selection of plants, trees, bushes, or root vegetables to be grown. Heavier, taller plants can be cultivated because of the support system that media-based beds offer.

Media based beds create ideal surfaces for mineralization to occur whereas water-based beds tend to be too diluted to allow the plants to gain the nourishment that they need. As the oxygenated water and excretions from the fish collect on the rocks (or whatever medium is chosen) in the bed, the natural cycle will begin to transform the chemical compounds into the nutrients plants so desperately need.

Another benefit of using media based beds is algae prevention. The media used like rocks block the light from hitting the roots of the plants whereas water-based systems do not have any natural shields. If the roots get attacked by algae, it impairs their ability to breathe, drink, and filter. Likewise, if the roots are exposed to direct light, they can get burnt and impair their ability to absorb water.

Also, an important function of media based beds, as mentioned earlier, is the filtration. Removing the media from the equation opens the doors for several issues. If waste is not removed from the fish tank, it is not only deadly to the fish but it can also cause blockage in the roots of the plants which will prevent them from eating and drinking.

They need water and nutrients to survive. For both the fish and plants, water-based systems require added filtration systems whereas media based beds eliminate the need because of their natural biofiltration process.

As I've said earlier, I aim to find a happy balance between form and function. Media beds allow for creativity, beauty, and a harmoniously functioning ecosystem to happen all in the same place. Koi ponds are great examples of this. Koi ponds have been designed with Aquaponics systems and amazing elements of design using media beds. They have beautiful plants and trees surrounding the pond and some even have plants on the pond, which make for a hybrid design of sorts. Incorporating Lily pads or other floating plants are elements of water-based systems. Additionally, waterfalls aid in biofiltration and water movement throughout the system and rock placement creates a beautiful environment.

The design you choose can be a real statement piece indoors or out and media based systems make it easier to do so, whereas, the need for filtration in water-based systems can be a real eyesore.

Obviously, media-based beds have many positive attributes but there are a few negatives that need to be mentioned for the sake of allowing you to make fully informed decisions as to which system you prefer for your personal Aquaponics garden.

As noted before, weight is certainly a factor to consider. Water alone is heavy but the addition of media such as rocks will increase the weight requirements of the area you choose, significantly.

Secondly, just like any filter, media beds can get clogged, which will cause a lack of oxygen to travel to the plants and ultimately to the fish. There are several indicators that will let you know that there is a potential threat from clogging:

• Rapid increase in pH

• Reduction in water flow through the bed

- Dense balls of roots have formed

Third, if the media used in the beds are not pH neutral or hasn't been rinsed first, a simple item like dirt or sand on the media might throw the pH levels out of balance.

Fourth, media doesn't just vary in assorted options, but it also varies in weight and cost.

It is very common for Aquaponics enthusiasts to select media such as:

- Gravel

- River rock

- Clay pellets

- Expanded shale

As far as price and availability, gravel is the least expensive, easy to obtain, and is beautiful for the garden, however, it is the heaviest option. Additionally, edges can be jagged and sharp, making it difficult to clean and arrange in beds without the use of thick protective gloves. River rocks are a good alternative since they have smooth edges but they are just as heavy. They are ideal for the support of heavier, taller plants.

The clay pellets are extremely lightweight but are much more difficult to find which results in a much more expensive purchase. Shale is very lightweight, weighing in slightly more than clay, and looks just like gravel. Shale is also in high demand and therefore carries a much higher price tag.

It is important to note, regardless of whether you purchase lightweight or heavier medium, media based grow beds will still be considerably weighty.

It is also important to stick to the dimensions advised. Anything smaller than ¾ inches will clog your system. It defeats the intention of the media bed altogether.

Water Based Grow Beds

There are two major ways of growing in water using Aquaponics:

- **DWC** (Deep Water Culture)

- **NFT** (Nutrient Film Technique)

We have discussed the benefits and drawbacks of media based beds and now we are going to explore the water-based grow beds and their pros and cons of use in Aquaponics. Before we discuss the two major ways to grow in water (DWC and NFT), we will look at the basics of water-based gardens.

Water-based gardening can be placed in locations that the heavier media based gardens simply could not go due to their weight restrictions. Because the roots of your plants are submerged, or partially submerged in water, there is no need for flooding and draining, and aside from occasional evaporation, water levels should remain consistent.

Water-based systems will require that filtration systems be put in place to remove fish solids and maintain proper levels for fish and plants. Plants will need to be in specialized containers for proper support. Because a filter is incorporated into the process to remove fish solids from clogging the plant roots which will prevent oxygen and nutrient absorption, it is absolutely imperative that proper nutrient rich mixtures be added to the environment. Also, filters require cleaning to ensure that they continue to work properly. In addition to the filter, it is important to add an aeration system to ensure adequate oxygen levels are achieved.

Nft

In Nutrient Film Technique, the plants will be handing over a water-filled container that the roots of the plant drop into in order to drink and eat. The water in these containers is shallow, as it is just enough for the roots to get what they need.

In an NFT system, it is important to maintain the same temperature for the water as you do for the growing area. Because of this, it is difficult to maintain these systems outdoors regardless of the season.

Dwc

In the Deep Water Culture system, the grow beds are flooded at all times. This system is much more productive than the NFT system. This system most closely resembles that of our ancestors, centuries ago, as it is a raft-like system of floating the plant holders in deep water.

Plumbing

Utilizing a kit versus DO IT YOURSELF does not require any plumbing knowledge and techniques, however, DO IT YOURSELF plumbing requires much more skill and knowledge.

Some things to keep in mind in DO IT YOURSELF and of course to be covered in an extensive DO IT YOURSELF manual, would be:

- Always be mindful of using products that are drinking water safe. If it says "non-potable", you cannot use it for the Aquaponics system. Did you know that garden hoses are not drinking water safe?
- Plumbing used to take water to the grow beds is often exposed to sunlight which can erode piping like PVC, which is the common piping choice due to its inexpensive cost.
- 90-degree angled piping will cause flow reduction and can have blockages occur due to water pressure and direction of flow.
- Be mindful of plumbing near electrical outlets. A leak could be extremely dangerous.
- Always keep in mind your plant and fish needs when developing your plumbing structures. Air and water are vital components and therefore the set up you choose for aeration, filtration, and water movement is of utmost importance to the life of the ecosystem you build.
- The entire amount of water in your system must be circulated hourly.
- An inexpensive way to ensure adequate oxygen supply is to have an air pump with a diffuser.

Water

326

Water makes the Aquaponics system go round. Literally, without water, the plants and fish could not survive. We cover some form of Biology in most of what we do in learning how to be successful in Aquaponics, but now it's time to discuss another area of science. Hold on and get onboard our time machine, we are going back to chemistry 101 class to get a brief review. I loved science, but Chemistry was not my favorite.

However, now that we are delving into the world of Aquaponics and creating our own ecosystem, the knowledge of basic chemistry becomes very important, especially when discussing water.

Without getting too heavy into chemical breakdowns and equations, this section will discuss the difference between acids, neutrals, and alkalis, so that we have a better understanding of pH balance.

Water (H2O) is a compound made up of two Hydrogen atoms and one Oxygen atom. In water, Hydrogen ions and Hydroxide ions are of equal counts in Water and were formed when molecules divided up. Those molecules that lost a hydrogen become known as Hydroxide ions and that little hydrogen that left the molecule, connected with water molecules to make Hydrogen ions. Because there is an equal balance of the two types of ions, water is neutral.

Once this balance is thrown off in either direction, we get an acid or a base, also known as an alkaline. When a substance is dissolved in water, it will either become acidic or basic (alkaline). An acid will demonstrate a higher amount of Hydrogen ions than Hydroxide ions when dissolved in water. The opposite is true of alkalis. A base is a solution with more Hydroxide ions than Hydrogen ions when it is dissolved in water.

We measure acidity and alkalinity with a pH scale. What does this mean? A one unit value on the pH scale corresponds to a change in Hydrogen ions multiplied by 10 for each value change. Water sits on the center of the pH scale at a value of 7. Basically, anything registering a value lower than water on the pH scale is considered Acids and anything registering values higher than water on the pH scale are considered bases or alkaline.

So that you can get an idea of what might register a pH value of an acid or a base in comparison to water, I have listed some acids and alkaline you might be familiar with below:

Acids

- Battery Acid (pH= 0)

- Vinegar (pH= 2)

- Orange Juice (pH= 3)

- Black Coffee; Bananas (pH= 5)

- Milk (pH= 6)

Alkalines

- Eggs (pH= 8)

- Baking Soda (pH= 9)

- Milk of Magnesia (pH= 10)

- Soapy Water (pH= 12)

- Liquid Drano (pH= 14)

So why is this chemistry lesson so important? Both acids and bases can cause a lot of damage. Plants thrive in an environment that has a pH levels registering anywhere between a value of 6 or 7.

Most people automatically think of acids as harmful substances, but bases contain a lot of salts and metals in them which can be highly corrosive. Distilled water is completely safe for your ecosystem as it is a neutral, pH value of 7. Due to the damaging effects that acids and bases can have on both your plants and your fish, and yes, even the plumbing and tank, it is extremely important that pH levels are tested regularly.

Water Weight

I use this excuse every time I get on the scale, but it is true, water weighs a lot! I mentioned this fact several times throughout the book so I will just touch upon this briefly here. Sometimes math can throw us for a loop, and like chemistry, math was not my favorite subject but it comes in handy in Aquaponics. Most people will automatically know how many gallons of water they may be able to fit in their tank or container but being aware of what each of those gallons weighs is very important. Did you know that one gallon of water is equivalent to eight pounds? Let's put those numbers in perspective. If you buy a 100-gallon tank to house your fish, this means that yes; it will hold 100 gallons of water. The tank full of water will then weigh approximately 1150 pounds! That is a major amount of weight and not every location can support this kind of weight and in Aquaponics gardens, water is not the only factor causing the scales to tip. Additionally, it is important to consider square footage in regards to weight. The dirt outside can actually withstand up to 200 pounds per square foot and a basement made of concrete flooring could withstand half that weight.

Water Temperature

The climate that your fish prefer plays an important role in their survival and growth. There are not many plants or fish that can adapt to varying habitats. Temperature is a key factor in ensuring an ideal environment for your ecosystem. Water, important to both fish and plants, is very sensitive to temperatures and can easily heat up or cool down due to intervention from an external source that comes in direct contact with it. Additionally, the plants and fish in your Aquaponic ecosystem need oxygen to thrive, and in fact, without it would perish. They get their oxygen from water. Did you know that temperature can affect the amount of oxygen that is dissolved in water and therefore how much oxygen the pants and fish are getting?

During warm days, as the sun beats down on your garden, everything is feeling the effects of the heat. You may not think about it, but the rocks hold a lot of heat, the plumbing holds in heat, and of course, the tank itself. When the water comes in contact with hot surfaces, it will absorb their heat, which will increase the temperature of the water.

Maintaining specific temperature ranges for your plants and fish in the ecosystem you created, is vital for it to thrive. In order to do so, use a thermometer specifically designed to measure water temperatures. It is important to check this on a daily basis, and if possible, several times per day.

For those that choose to automate, this is one of those areas that I would recommend having an automated monitor because it will alert you the moment the temperatures rise or drop out of proper range. Temperature fluctuations happen constantly throughout the course of a day, whether your garden is inside or out, it will feel those changes. Not all fluctuations will be enough to make a difference that will knock temperatures out of range, however, keeping an eye on this is very important. If you live in an area where you don't experience a change in seasons, it's a bit easier avoiding drastic temperature changes, but for those of us that do experience the four seasons, extra measures, pardon the pun, need to be taken. Here are some suggestions:

- Whether you are heading into the hot summer months or the freezing winter months, insulation is a great way to moderate temperatures. Keep in mind that there are different types of insulation. In order to keep the pipes from getting too much heat exposure, an insulation that has a reflective outer shield is recommended. Other types of insulation (without reflective shield) would work well to maintain normal temperatures and keep pipes from freezing. It is also suggested that tanks and/or containers have insulation if outdoors during the colder months and adding extra rocks (or other media) to your grow beds will help give them additional insulation.
- If your garden is outdoors and exposed to the elements of seasonal changes, it would help to put a temporary covering over the area, giving it a greenhouse effect.
- When water is moving, the energy produced is converted to heat and therefore will be less likely to freeze. To keep water movement constant, make sure to run your air pump at all times.

- Maintaining a constant flow of water through the use of an air pump will additionally ensure that oxygen is circulating throughout your system.

Evaporation and Condensation

Warm, dry air attracts moisture and cold air repels it. When your tank water is exposed to the thirsty warm air, the air will start to drink from the tank. When the water disappears from the tank into the air it is called evaporation. Differences in temperatures can react in other ways. If the air is colder than your garden, it will cause moisture from the air to be released and build upon area surfaces outside of your garden like perhaps a window. If your garden is cooler than the air, this effect known as condensation will occur right in your garden.

Remember, it is important to maintain balance in the ecosystem you create, so both conditions should be avoided as they can affect temperature fluctuations as well as dissolved oxygen levels. I will discuss dissolved oxygen shortly but first, let's discuss ways in which you can deal with evaporation and condensation.

- Having a thermometer that measures the humidity is a good start.

- Try to reduce how much water is exposed to the air. Placing a cover over the tank or container would help minimize exposure.

- You can cover areas of water in the grow beds as well by simply adding an additional couple of inches of media.

The amount of natural evaporation that occurs in the Aquaponics garden will only be about 1/10 of the amount that would occur in a soil grown garden so top off your tank water to maintain optimal water levels. Remember, you never have to replace the water in Aquaponics because doing so would waste all the natural nutrients produced in that water.

The water temperature has a profound effect on the activity and behavior of fish. It also affects their feeding habits, growth rates, and reproduction.

As I mentioned earlier, water temperatures affect oxygen levels, which are not just important to fish but are also important to the plants and bacteria in your Aquaponic ecosystem. In order for aquatic creatures to get the oxygen they need, it must be dissolved in water. When those dissolved oxygen levels are lower than a reading of 5, fish in your garden will become stressed. The closer that reading comes to 2 and the longer it remains in that vicinity, stress is increased and the death of the fish will be imminent.

How do temperatures affect the dissolved oxygen levels? Warmer temperatures of water are saturated by oxygen and as a result, can hold less oxygen; therefore, the dissolved oxygen levels are lower. Colder temperatures of water are the opposite; therefore, the dissolved oxygen levels are higher.

This conversation always reminds me of the three little bears and Goldilocks. One is too hot. One is too cold. Well, the fish want it "just right" also. Let's look at dissolved oxygen and temperature another way. In warmer water environments, fish metabolism speeds up, so the fish require more oxygen, but warmer water has low dissolved oxygen levels. As you can imagine, if the fish are desperately in need of oxygen, they begin to get erratic, kind of like someone who is drowning, they act panicked. In colder water environments, the metabolism of the fish slows down, so they need less oxygen, however, cold water has a higher level of dissolved oxygen. The high levels cause the fish to be tired and sleepy, which affects feeding habits and reproduction.

If your levels are low, in addition to monitoring and controlling temperatures to avoid issues with oxygen levels, using an aeration system will help to add oxygen to both the fish tank and the grow beds. When levels are high, it may be time to add more grow beds since the plants share the oxygenated water with the fish.

Adding plants mean more life using the oxygen and thus dissolved oxygen levels should decrease. Aside from your oxygen monitors reflecting a change in oxygen levels, you should see a change in behavior of your aquatic species.

Light

Light is essential to the well being of plants and for that reason, just as it is important to know about water, temperature, nutrients, and oxygen (vital knowledge to have in order to maintain a thriving ecosystem), it is equally important to understand the many facets of light, the difference in light sources, and how these variables affect life in your Aquaponics garden.

There is obviously a big difference between growing indoors and outdoors when it comes to light, and though there are natural advantages of the sun's light outdoors, there are still things that need to be taken into consideration when growing outside. This section will discuss proper lighting for both indoor Aquaponics and outdoor Aquaponics gardening.

Plants have a molecule called Chlorophyll which takes light and changes it into energy that the plants can absorb. Because the plants feed off the energy produced by light to grow, having the proper lighting is a must for them to thrive. Different plants require different amounts of light (called lumens) and different plants respond to different colors of light (called wavelengths).

Amount

First, it is important to recognize that the light people process with their eyes to see, is very different from the light plants need to process for their energy requirements. The wavelengths plants use are red and/or blue and are known as photosynthetically active radiation referred to by its acronym PAR.

To figure out the optimal PAR quantity for your indoor garden plants, you must consider four things:

- Distance of light to plants

- Type of bulb

- Type of light fixture

- Amount of natural light present

335

If your garden is outside in direct sunlight, it is receiving 100,000 lux (lumens per square meter). Not all plants thrive in direct sun exposure like a cactus. Most plants require 20,000 lux which is what they would get on a day with normal clear conditions. Regular indoor lights found in a kitchen or office, may produce 400 lux. These differences alone explain why proper lighting conditions are so important. In an Aquaponics garden, a variety of plants can be grown at the same time and though you may have all warm weather plants or all cold climate plants, requiring the same temperatures and lighting, the height of the plants can also make a difference. A tall plant in the wrong location may block light from getting to some of the shorter plants. Because Aquaponics uses grow beds versus soil, you can easily rearrange the plants in your garden to ensure they all get the light they need.

Artificial lighting known as grow lights are a serious blessing but there are so many options out there and the price is not the only factor to consider. Dependent on the amount of area you need to light and which bulbs that you use, you will need to figure out how many of that particular bulb it will take to release the sufficient amount of energy the plants in your garden require. For example, if you have a 16 sq ft area garden, you would need only one high-intensity discharge HPS bulb of 400 watts. But if you chose to use fluorescent light bulbs, you would need five of the 125 watt compact to grow lights, ten of the high output 54 watt lights, or forty-two of the 40 watt standard fluorescent lights. You would need twice as many standard white 60 watt light bulbs than standard fluorescent.

Obviously, you would probably vote for buying and using fewer bulbs but you also need to consider price and how often you would need to replace them. Though fluorescent lighting requires more bulbs, the lighting fixture and the bulbs are relatively inexpensive, energy efficient, and take up a smaller amount of space.

The issue is that they need to be replaced after only six months in order to get proper PAR for your garden. Also, fluorescents are not a highly effective PAR for denser gardens.

High-intensity discharge bulbs work the best and most closely resemble the light given off by the sun, however, it is expensive and so are the fixtures. Additionally, they are energy intensive and emit a lot of heat.

Chapter 5: Nutrient Cycle & Bacteria

Well, if you thought your science lesson was over, you were definitely mistaken. Chemistry 101 continues as we delve deeper into Aquaponics. It is time to learn about a major part of the circle of life in our Aquaponics system. Many seem to forget about this process and how it works when they attempt to simply define how exactly Aquaponics works.

I imagine the same is true for how cow manure fertilizes the crops. How many people have actually thought about how and why manure actually helps the crops grow? I know I never gave it a second thought. I just knew it worked. Well, in Aquaponics it is extremely important to know how to fish poop feeds your plants. Because we are essentially creating an ecosystem, for the ecosystem to function like a natural ecosystem, we have to help it out and play "mother nature" in our garden. How can we help our fish to help our plants to help our fish?

Well, Mother Nature does her job so efficiently that we don't think a lot about the inner workings and intricacies behind nature and how it is able to thrive. Hopefully, by the time you are done with not just this chapter, but this book, you will have a much better grasp and ability to help nature take its course in the Aquaponics ecosystem you create.

Ammonia, Nitrites, and Nitrates

Nitrogen is extremely important to the life of plants and through nitrogen is found in the air we breathe, it is not in a form that is usable to plants, so plants need to get their necessary nitrogen from an alternate source.

Through the use of an Aquaponics system, plants can get nitrogen in the form that's suitable to them. This form of nitrogen is called Nitrate and it is made by bacteria that process Ammonia in order to grow. These bacteria are known as beneficial bacteria because they help achieve a positive outcome. Penicillin falls in this category. The more beneficial bacteria there is, the better it will be for your ecosystem because the fish release ammonia constantly through their waste and through their gills.

The bacteria eat the fish waste and process it, turning ammonia into nitrates for the plants to get fertilized.

When you first start your Aquaponics system, there are specific stages you take in which plants and fish are introduced.

Before both, you will simply have water that will not only be used to test and make sure the system flows properly, but also to test for temperatures, oxygen, pH, and other balances. One of these tests which you will run periodically is to test for ammonia, nitrites, and nitrates. Obviously, we can't see bacteria because they are microscopic, so this test is very important. You might be thinking at this point:

- How can we be testing for something that comes out of fish when there are no fish?

- How can we introduce plants before fish, when fish feed the plants?

Both are good questions. Water in the tank right now will show no ammonia, no nitrites, and no nitrates, which as the question above pointed out, is a problem for the plants.

It is not only a problem for the plants but also for the good bacteria we want to grow in our tank. If there is no ammonia, there will be no bacteria. As I said, this is a circle of life and we play Mother Nature so we must intervene and add ammonia so that there is a food source for bacteria. We essentially step in as substitutes for the fish until they can assume the role on a regular basis. We must monitor the process regularly and once we get to a level that works for our plants, then we can introduce them to the system.

In the meantime, as we add ammonia, bacteria appear and start to do their job of converting it to nitrate. Our measurements will gradually show a decline in ammonia and a rise in nitrites. This is the level between ammonia and nitrates.

Bacteria are doing its thing, but we are not quite there yet. Next, measurements will show a decrease further in ammonia, a decrease in nitrate, and now an increase in nitrate. Soon our measurements will reflect the necessary nitrate levels to effectively fertilize our plants and this means that bacteria levels are growing. This is good news and should only take about two weeks to achieve. This bacterial process is known as cycling. You know that your garden is fully cycled when there is a continual process of transforming ammonia into nitrite into nitrate.

The addition of fish should maintain a fully cycled system.

Let us go back to the question about fish being introduced after plants. You could technically add plants and fish simultaneously as long as the ammonia levels have officially dropped to zero. Ammonia is poisonous to fish and though they are the ones producing it, they cannot live in it. Fish in an aquarium would have a filter to remove waste products to keep levels safe but in Aquaponics, we need to rely on the bacteria and the plants to keep the water safe for the fish.

Ammonia kits will advise proper levels and amount to add to your tank to ignite bacteria production and eventually nitrate. As each level is achieved through the cycle, less ammonia should be added. Generally, liquid ammonia is used and administered with a dropper. Another way to increase ammonia levels is to drop a few dead fish in the water since decomposing organisms release ammonia.

The intermediary level of the cycle, nitrite, usually occurs in the second week of the process. Though it is not quite as lethal as ammonia, it is important to continue measuring these levels until you reach the third level, nitrate, where it is beneficial to plants and safe for fish. During this nitrite cycle, do not add fish because nitrites stop blood from oxygen absorption and can cause gastrointestinal, renal, and nervous system failures.

Because oxygen absorption is prevented, fish can stop breathing regardless of the oxygen supply available in their water.

Plants and fish will both benefit from the nitrate level of the cycle. Once your plants are consuming the nitrates, and you are in full cycle, your measurements may reflect zero on all three levels of the cycle once again: ammonia, nitrite, and nitrate.

Mineralization

The process by which chemical compounds are broken down in organic matter for plants to utilize is known as mineralization. The media surfaces of your garden are highly conducive to this process since the water and waste

from the tank flows through their regularly, allowing for the transformation into minerals and nutrients to occur naturally.

Other Additives

Ammonia is added to achieve cycling but there are other things you could add to help your plants flourish. Adding chelated iron powder will help the plants convert light to energy and look vibrant and full. Another additive would be kelp or seaweed because they have a host of vitamins and minerals needed by plants.

Chapter 6: How To Do It Yourself

Though it can be time-consuming and a bit daunting at times, it is extremely rewarding to be able to say you did it yourself and yes, it works! Believe me, it will be so worth it, in the end, knowing that you did your part for the environment and have the ability to successfully sustain your family through the food cultivated in an Aquaponics garden that you created with your bare hands!

Okay, so let's get started creating the environment for your own Aquaponic ecosystem. The main components of this ecosystem structure are the fish tank or tanks, the grow bed(s), and plumbing. Having the correct pieces for the puzzle and putting them together properly is vital for the living elements of your garden to flourish.

As you have read in the previous chapters, there are several options to choose from for your set up and functionality. This chapter will cover all of those options and functions so that you have the details needed to create your Aquaponic ecosystem as you wish to.

The first thing to consider is the fish tank. It is important to determine whether you want to start big or small. If you want a small system, then a regular aquarium of about 10 or 20 gallons would suffice. If you want to go for the gold and go big, you need something with the capacity to contain a few hundred gallons of water, at least. This is not determined by what you wish to do with the fish (whether you are eating them or not), but how large a production of vegetables, herbs, and/or fruits you wish to have.

Remember that no matter the size, any piece used in this puzzle must meet the standards of food/drinking water safety. If you do happen to find an aquarium that meets your capacity and cost requirements, you will need to take added measures to protect its inhabitants. First, it is wise to have a tank cover and secondly, additional filtration and aeration must be used to assist the plants in keeping the fish happy and healthy. These added items will protect them from algae, reduced oxygen levels, and overexposure (to light sources and peering eyes).

Some people choose to avoid the added expenses of the aquarium set up and enjoy taking on do it yourself to the level of building everything from scratch, increasing the amount of work and time involved for sure, but also the level of creative freedom. This avenue will allow for more control over your piggy bank as well as how much recycling and reusing actually gets incorporated into this process. There are numerous items you can use to build your tank and grow beds such as plastic barrels, IBC's, stock tanks, bathtubs, fish pond containers, and more. The list is long but what you choose depends on needs, size, whether you are indoors or out, appearance, cost, ability to locate specific supplies and ability to transport those supplies. So many variables!

Some Options:

One popular money-saving option is to use plastic barrels, otherwise known as 55-gallon drums. Though there are several color options for these however blue is the ideal option for the Aquaponics gardener due to its ability to block sun exposure and because blue barrels are specifically made to carry food products which makes it safe to use for your system.

These barrels can be used for both the fish tank and the garden grow beds so they will need to be cut accordingly which means you will need to break out the jigsaw. As an option, these items are easy to find and easy to transport due to size and weight. Though they are not pretty to look at, they can be used inside or out. Some people choose to decorate the exterior when using indoors.

Another option is the IBC (Intermediate Bulk Container).

- Holds 275 gallons or more

- Wrapped in a metal cage

- Much more difficult to transform to a fish tank, sump tank, or grow bed—heavy duty tools needed!

- 48 inches tall on average

- Takes up a lot of yard space

- Need a truck to transport

- IBC tote kits are available at Aquaponics store

- To make building easier, you can visit backyardaquaponics.com to learn how

Stock tanks are made from sturdy plastic and can be found at agriculture or hardware chain stores.

- Considerably less expensive than an aquarium of the equivalent size which would cost about ten times more

- Fit in an SUV or van versus needing a truck

- Only 25 inches tall, making it ideal for the multilevel capability of grow beds over tanks and ease of access

- Can be purchased in assorted sizes

- A 50-gallon stock tank is usually about 12 inches high, which is an ideal height requirement for your garden grow beds

- The rounded shape of the stock tank is ideal for water circulation removing the ability to have dead zones that would likely occur in a rectangular aquarium set up

Specialty tanks like pond shells are made specifically for fish to thrive and can have over 1000 gallons in capacity.

Additionally, they can be specially made with viewing areas so that you can see your fish. This can be a great option however it is important to consider that retailers in the United States are scarce still when it comes to Aquaponic specific items and therefore prices and shipping can be high.

As I stated earlier, the options are many and after you read this book or physically build your first system, you may come up with your own ingenious, creative ideas on how to set up your Aquaponics garden. You will have the knowledge to do so with confidence.

I will discuss how to create your system using stock tanks and also show you how to do so with plastic barrels in two formats: with sump pump and without. One format is a vertical, more compact set up that doesn't require a stand, and saves space, and the other format is a side by side setup that takes up more area. Keep in mind, when setting any Aquaponics system indoors, you must add proper lighting and maintain proper temperatures.

Weight also needs to be taken into consideration. For your outdoor setups, you may want to consider some type of coverage like a greenhouse for added protection from the elements and pests. Another note if you want to cultivate plants which need to grow high and/or wide, you need to provide additional support and structures.

Considering a pergola may be a good idea and they are not difficult to build if you prefer not to purchase one.

Here are some specifics on the various parts you would use:

Bulkhead Fittings & Standpipes

Bulkhead fittings are used in plumbing done specifically in liquid storage. They are made so that a connection can pass through a watertight wall. These items have three main components: The threaded male part that projects through the watertight wall, also known as a bulkhead; The threaded female part that screws onto the male part; and a gasket to form enough pressure to prevent leakage. A bulkhead fitting is purposely made to allow pipes to connect from to another for water passage. The standpipe is a pipe that is vertical and extends from a supply of water. This pipe is placed inside the bulkhead fitting. As the water rises in the grow bed, where your standpipe is placed and reaches the top of the standpipe, the water will flow over it and out of the grow bed.

Uniseal

Uniseal is a rubber O shaped gasket that fits right into a hole and can be used as an alternative to the bulkhead fitting accomplishing the same task of passing piping through a watertight seal.

PVC

PVC is the most commonly used piping for plumbing because it is inexpensive, easy to work with, and easy to find.

Irrigation Poly Tubing

Irrigation Poly Tubing is a very durable tubing used in irrigation however most cases not used in plumbing and therefore not safe for drinking water. Finding an exception in this category could prove very difficult.

Garden Hose

Garden hoses can be a great use for Aquaponics however you must be mindful of which hoses are non potable, like the green ones which are very toxic. If you purchase the hose in 5/8" diameter, it will coincide with most of the fittings you have in your system and it is flexible so allows you to run it easily from one place to another.

Vinyl Tubing

Black vinyl tubing is another great option for plumbing, however it is important to note that it needs to be securely attached to something, due to its tendency to move around when water pressure flows through it.

Corrugated Tubing

Corrugated tubing is the fancy looking black vinyl tubing that has coils in it to prevent kinking. This tubing is very common and easy to find.

Air Pumps

Air pumps come in many capacities however your Aquaponics system will need a specific air volume so purchasing one should be based on this criterion as opposed to water volume. These pumps are vital components to your system as they add much-needed oxygen to the water in your tank while circulating the water, which is also very important for the fish. I suggest purchasing one that has numerous outlets for more air flow.

Diffusers

Diffusers are made to divide the air that flows from the air pump producing smaller bubbles and a wider area of air coverage. Air stones and line diffusers are popular types of diffusers used in Aquaponics systems.

Water Pumps

Generally speaking, submersible water pumps are used in home Aquaponics systems. When purchasing a water pump, you need o make sure that the pump has the ability to circulate the entire volume of water in your Aquaponics system, every hour on the hour. The more powerful the better and though pumps are made for aquariums, it is more likely that you will get the proper pump if you purchase from a store that specializes in hydroponics or aquaponics. One last note would be that you should always remove the mesh filter from the pump to allow adequate flow.

SLO

A solids lifting overflow is a type of standpipe that will remove the debris from the bottom of the fish tank while maintaining consistent water levels.

Timers

This a device to turn things on and off and can be set for automatic time frames and apply to flood and drain, lighting, and more. Specialty stores will carry ones that can be programmed to repeat cycles.

Indexing Valve

Used in conjunction with a timer that has repeat cycles, the indexing valve will move the flow of water from one inlet to many outlets and is commonly used when there are multiple grow beds. These valves based on settings will allow flow to one bed at a time and as one is done, it will close that outlet and open another.

Auto Siphon

An auto siphon is made to automatically drain a container when the fluid level rises above the rim of the siphon and requires no electricity. The most popular siphons used are loop configuration and bell configuration. When using a loop siphon configuration, tubing is looped from the bottom of the media bed to the point at which you want the flood and drain to occur.

When using the bell siphon configuration, the bell is placed over the standpipe itself and drains once the water reaches the top. Basically, a siphon occurs when the water overflows the standpipe and drains until air enters the bottom of the bell breaking the cycle of the siphon. The Affnan bell siphon has a funnel shape at the top to increase the amount of water flowing through the siphon. Coanda drains are also used in the siphon process since it connects the lower section with the drain section using a 45-degree connector causing the water flow to remain high and reduce obstruction.

Here are some options for system design:

Aquaponics Design #1: 100-Gallon Stock Tank System

Supplies Needed:

- (2) 10-foot kiln dried 2x6 planks

- (2) 50-gallon stock tanks

- (1) 100-gallon stock tank

- (1) 1 x 3 board

- (1) 2 x 3 board

- (12) 8 x 8 x 16 concrete blocks

- (2) bulkhead fittings

- (2) Coanda drains with 2-inch lengths of PVC
- (2) Affnan-style standpipes
- (2) bell assemblies (2" PVC pipe and 2" PVC cap)
- (2) media guards
- (1) 25-foot 5/8" hose that is drinking water safe
- (2) female hose fittings
- (1) 400 gph (gallon per hour) water pump
- (1) plastic hose splitter
- (1) roll synthetic twine
- (1) air stone
- (1) ¼" vinyl air tubing
- (1) air check valve
- (1) small air pump
- 13 cubic feet of rocks from quarry

Tools Needed:

- Permanent Marker
- 1" spade drill bit, ¼" bit, and drill
- Miter saw

• Scissors

Start by preparing the frame. Place the two 2x6 planks on the
ground about 4" apart. Place one of the 50-gallon grows
beds on the planks, bottom side down. Mark, where the
bottom of the grow bed, hits the planks to determine where
to cut. Move the grow bed over about 4 feet and mark the
planks again.

Cut the planks with the miter saw and set aside. Trim the 2x6
scraps pieces so that they are 16 inches in length. Trim the
1x3 board and the 2x3 board into as many 16 inch pieces as
you can. Next, position the fish tank and grow bed support
system. Place the 100-gallon tank in the center of your
space where it will be permanently positioned.

Create two stacks of three concrete block stacks. Shim the planks
with the 16 inch long boards you have cut. Next cut the holes
in the grow beds to insert fittings. You will do this by
turning the 50-gallon stock tanks upside down. Make a hole
for the standpipe in the middle near one end using the 1"
spade bit in the drill. The hole should be drilled in the
bottom of each 50-gallon stock tank.

Assemble the bulkheads, Coanda drains, and standpipes in the
beds. Assemble the bulkhead fittings in the hole through the
bin. Put the male conduit connector through the whole first
then slide the O-ring over the male pipe threads and then
screw on the female conduit fitting.

Stick the Coanda drain into the bottom of the bulkhead fittings.
Stick the Affnan-style standpipe into the top of the
bulkhead fitting. A 5 1/2" PVC pipe is a good length for
connecting the fittings to the bulkhead. Position the 50-
gallon stock tanks on the planks so the water will drain into

the fish tank. These will be your grow beds. Place the PVC bell assemblies over the standpipes and slide the media guards over the bell portion of the standpipe drain.

Assemble the water pump and tubing. Cut the hose about 2 feet away from the male fitting. Cut two more lengths of hose about 7 feet long. Attach the cut end of the short hose to the pump. If the pump has a mesh or foam filter pad inside, remove it. Attach the hose splitter to the male end of the hose connected to the pump. Connect the female hose fittings to each of the 7-foot hose sections. Connect the 7-foot hose sections to the hose splitter. Make sure the splitter levers are turned in a direction that allows water to flow out.

Connect the hose to the fish tank and grow beds. Use the twine to connect the splitter to the fish tank. Use the twine to fasten the hoses so they will add water to the far end of each grows bed. You want the water coming in at the opposite side of the grow beds from where it will drain out. The length of twine should be sufficient enough to tie the hose along the side of the grow bed.

Assemble the air pump, tubing, and air stone by pushing the air stone onto the ¼" tubing. Clip a small portion of the tubing to use later on. Push the other end of the short length of tubing onto the opposite end of the check valve. Next, push the free portion of short tubing onto the air pump and place the air stone into the fish tank.

It's time to add media and water and turn the system on to conduct testing. First, rinse the stones one bucket at a time and add the rinsed stones to the grow beds. Add water to the system and turn the pumps on, adjusting the levers on the hose splitters to reduce the flow rate if necessary.

If the flow rate is too high, your siphon cycle won't break. Once you see that everything is working properly and water tests are reading properly, you can move forward with plants and fish. This system should hold up to 15 fish at around a pound each when matured.

Aquaponics Design #2: Plastic Barrel

Supplies Needed:

- (1) 55-gallon BLUE barrel

- (1) 200 gph water pump

- Grow Medium

- (1) T fitting

- ½" PVC piping

- (2) #18 O-rings for grow bed connections

- (2) #14 O-rings for intake connections

- (1) ¾" PVC pipe 6" long for bell siphon

- (2) ¾" 90-degree elbow for the drain pipe

- (2) ¾" PVC pipe 4" long

- (1) ¾" male adapter threaded to slip for grow bed connections

- (1) ¾" female adapter threaded to slip for grow bed connections

- (1) ½" male adapter threaded to slip for intake connections

- (1) ½" female adapter threaded to slip for intake connections

- (1) ¾" to 1 ½" Bell Adapter

- (1) 2" PVC pipe 10" long for bell dome

- (1) 2" PVC pipe cap for bell dome

- (1) 3" PVC pipe 12" long for gravel guard

Tools Needed:

- Anything you prefer to use to cut holes into plastic PVC and slice barrels, like a Drill, Dremel or jigsaw

- 1/8" Drill bit

- 100% silicone and caulk gun

- Sandpaper (or rotary filing tool like a Bur)

- Sharpie

The barrel needs to be cut into two parts. Lay the barrel on its side and measure 12 inches from the top to cut around the barrel and remove one-third of it for the grow beds. The bottom two-thirds remaining will be used for the fish tank. After cutting, you want to smooth the edges with either sandpaper or a Bur, if you have one. Once you have smoothed the cut areas, wash out the barrels for added safety measures.

On the grow bed portion of your set up, you will need to make holes for the bell siphon and intake hose.

Flip the bottom of the grow bed portion upside down and make your diameter measurements to match the actual parts being used. Once you have determined the size that the holes need to be to ensure a snug fit around pipes and hoses, use the Dremel to drill out your desired holes.

Make sure you set the two holes on opposite sides of the grow bed container. Once holes are made, smooth out the cut surface.

Next, you will need to measure two holes to be cut in the fish tank portion of the barrel. One hole will be for fish viewing and access and the other hole will be for the power cord of the water pump. Some barrels have markings on them that tell you where the 30-gallon mark would be. If the barrel that you have purchased does not have this marking, simply measure about 16 ¾" from the bottom of the fish tank.

This will be where you mark your water line. The next step will be to determine what shape you want for your viewing window. Some people have used fish or whale shapes, but an oval or circle will work just fine. Use a pre-made template or plastic plate to ensure that you outline the cutting line with a sharpie exactly the size and shape you wish.

Remember to make sure that you set this area above the water level and leave a bit of space from the top as well (maybe two inches for both). Once you have done this, use your jigsaw, Dremel or whatever tool works for you, and cut out the viewing area. The next hole will be smaller since it is simply for cord passage, maybe the size of a plastic soup bowl. This hole will also need to be placed above the water zone. This should be followed by smoothing out the rough areas of your cut outs.

In order to attach the grow bed portion to the fish tank portion, you will need to make eight small holes that are equally spaced out around the very top of the fish tank.

This will be attached to the grow bed with zip ties so that gives you an idea of diameter of the holes, but also means that you must place eight small holes on the lip at the bottom of the grow bed that line up exactly to the fish tank holes. Once you have done this, run the zip ties through each hole and tighten the grow bed to the fish tank. Cut the excess zip tie section off after you have secured everything together.

Now that the frame is built, you need to install the plumbing mechanisms. In order to do so, you will start by building your bell siphon. Take the male adapter and slip a #18 o-ring over the threads. Insert the adapter through the access hole that you have made in your grow bed.

Slip another #18 o-ring over the top of the male threads. Screw the female and male adapters together ensuring that there is a tight connection. Slip a four to a six-inch piece of ¾" PVC pipe into the female adapter. The length will be determined by the water height so start at six and cut down to four if necessary. Slip the ¾" to 1 ½" bell adapter on top of the ¾" PVC pipe. To create an effective drain flow, it is important that the opening of the Bell is double the size of the pipe. Slide the PVC bell dome, 10" (can be adjusted to a shorter length if need be), over the drain pipe and the PVC gravel guard over this.

For the side of the grow bed facing the fish, slide a piece of ¾" pipe into the bottom of the male adapter. Slide a ¾" PVC pipe and 90-degree elbow into the bottom of this pipe and then repeat with another ¾" PVC pipe and another 90-degree elbow.

The next step is to build the intake mechanism. Just as you did for the bell siphon, you will make a watertight seal in the hole you created using the male and female adapters, ½" this time, and the #14 O-rings. Place the water pump in the bottom of the fish tank (run the electrical cord out of the rear hole you created) and connect it to the bottom of the ½" adapter with a piece of ½" PVC pipe.

The pump line will run about ten inches into the top of the intake adapter in the grow bed. Attach this to a T fitting and cap any openings. It is important to drill a tiny hole into the horizontal section of the pipe to let some water out. Check the flow rate when testing and add another tiny hole or two, if necessary.

Now that your plumbing is in place, you will run the system with the water in the tank and check the intake flow rate, drain rate, and potential leaks. If the bungee holes have leaks, seal the leaks with the silicon. Once you are satisfied that your system is working correctly, you can add your medium to the grow bed and test for blockages.

Once all of this is complete, you may then move on to cycling the system for the proper introduction of your plants and fish.

Aquaponics Garden #3 Plastic Barrel with Stand, Sump, and Lighting

Supplies needed:

- 10 feet of one inch PVC

- 3 feet of three inch PVC cut into two eighteen inch lengths

- (4) slip elbows for one inch PVC

- (1) T fitting for one inch PVC

- (2) end caps for one inch PVC

- (2) eight foot 2x6 pressure treated wood that should be cut into (6) thirty-inch lengths

- (2) eight foot 2x8 pressure treated wood that should be cut into (6) thirty-inch lengths

- (4) ten foot 2x4 pressure treated wood that should be cut into (4)64-inch lengths and (4) 33-inch lengths

- (2) ten foot 2x4 pressure treated wood that should be cut into (4) 54 ½" inch lengths

- (2) eight foot 1x2 pressure treated wood that should be cut into (4) 48-inch lengths

- (4) sixty-inch lengths of metal chain

- (2) twelve-inch lengths of metal chain

- (4) S-hooks

- 300 gph water pump

- 20 feet of ½" flexible non-toxic tubing (drinking water safe)

- Metal Clamps

- Metal C-clamp

- (2) forty-eight-inch fluorescent shop lights with plugs

- (2) cool forty-eight-inch bulbs

- (2) warm forty-eight-inch bulbs

- (8) cinder blocks

- Twine

- Box of 2" deck screws

- Power Strip

- Timer

- Aquarium aerator with four nozzles

- (4) air stones

- 20 feet of airline tubing

- (2) ¾" to ½" tubing barb bulkhead fittings

- (1) Uniseal for 1" PVC

- Aquarium heater for 100-gallon tank

- (4) BLUE plastic barrels

- A ¼ cubic yard of Kenlite (or another medium)

Tools Needed:

- Power Drill

- Drill bit ¼"

- Drill hole saw bit 1.75" and 1.375"

- Jig Saw

The first step in the building process is to prepare the blue barrels. Each barrel has a different purpose and therefore needs to be prepared differently. The first barrel will be prepared for use as a fish tank. To start, lay the barrel on its side and cut a rectangular hole in the center measuring 13" x 23". Next, you will need to drill a hole on the circular side of the barrel using a 1.75" hole saw.

The hole should be located approximately 4" from the lip of the barrel and lined up with the hole that you cut on the side. Make sure any rough edges are smoothed. Make sure to wash the barrels. Place the 1" Uniseal through the hole.

Next, you will need to cut the rectangular window in the side of the barrel for the sump tank as well. It is important that both the fish tank barrel and the sump tank barrel have securely plugged bungholes, due to the fact that they will be containing water and you want to avoid leaks. The third barrel is going to be used for the grow beds so you just need to cut the barrel in half, lengthwise. Measure 1 inch from the lip of the barrel and drill a hole, with the 1.375 holes saw bit, on the bottom of each of these halves.

Thread the barbed bulkhead fitting through the hole in each. Attach it so that the ½" barbed fitting is on the outside of the half tank and make sure that the bulkhead is flush on the inside. The last tank will be used as a water reserve for topping off evaporated water in your system. For this, simply remove the top. It will remain standing upright. The water will be aerated and transferred as needed over time.

The next thing you will need to prepare is the frame that will hold the tanks and grow beds. Two of each length of 2x4 boards need to be combined. Use the deck screws to secure two 2x4's together to achieve 4x4's in length of 33, 54.5, and 64 inches. Create a V shape by attaching the 30-inch 2x6 boards and 30-inch 2x8 boards using deck screws.

The mouth of the V created should be about ten inches in width. You will need to build 6 altogether. Position three of the V's face down (one on each end and one in the center) onto the 54.5 inches long 4x4, about 12 inches apart, to create the grow bed stand. Next, lay out the two 30 inch pieces of lumber so that they are parallel to each other, about 30 inches apart. With the V facing down, position one on each end and attach them to the 54.5-inch boards using the deck screws.

Drill the screws through the outer edge of the V into the board on both sides. This will be used as the fish tank stand. Cinder blocks need to be set up at the corners of an area measuring 36 x 56 inches. Place the second set of cinder blocks on top of these. Take the 64 inch 4x4's and place them the 56-inch length of the area on the cinder blocks. The grow bed stand will sit atop of the 64 inch 4x4 with Vs facing forward. This should be flush at the edge of the 64 inch 4x4 putting the grow bed stands towards the front portion of the 64 inch 4x4.

The fish tank stand will be placed at the back end of the 64 inch 4x4 with the V's perpendicular to the grow beds, flush to the back edge of 64 inch 4x4. Position a 48-inch length of 1x2 to the corner of the grow bed stand, keeping the bottom of the board flush with the bottom of the 54.5 inch 4x4. The 2-inch width of the board should be along the 30-inch side of the grow bed stand. Use deck screws to attach the board in place. Do this to all four corners. Attach a single screw to the top of each of this 1x2's with a small portion of the screw sticking out for light fixtures to attach to later on.

Now that the frame has been built, you can place the grow beds and the fish tank on their respective stands with the V's as support structures. The sump tank will be placed on the floor in front of the grow bed stand and supported by the remaining V facing down.

Now, it's time to work on the plumbing. Cut a short section of 1 inch PVC pipe, approximately 3 inches in length. Push this section through the Uniseal in the fish tank so that only 1-inch sticks into the tank with the remainder sticking out. Add an L connector to the end of this piece so that the next PVC pipe will go straight down along the side of the tank. Cut another piece of PVC approximately 4 inches in length and attach it to the L connector, ending about midway down the height of the fish tank. Add another L connector to the end of this piece to change the direction to head towards the Grow Beds.

Cut a 4-inch section of PVC to slip into the L connector and travel beyond the edge of the fish tank. Add another L connector to the end of this piece to change the direction to wrap around the midsection of the tank. This will make the next piece of PVC travel along the length of the fish tank. Cut a 16-inch length of PVC and fit it into the L connector. This piece should end roughly near the midpoint of the long dimension of the fish tank. Add a final L connector to the end of the PVC to change the direction to point away from the fish tank and towards the grow beds. Cut a final 4-inch section of PVC and slip it into the L.

It should end over the Grow Beds, running between the two halves. Add a T connector to the end of the pipe to split the flow between the two grow beds. If necessary, add a short section of PVC to each side of the T so that water flows into the grow beds rather than into the space between the two beds.

Using a ¼" drill bit, drill a hole into the end wall of each grow bed half barrel tank near the upper edge. This should be on the same side near the bulkhead fitting sticking out of the bottom. Attach a 24-inch section of ½" black vinyl tubing onto the barbed end of the bulkhead fitting in the grow bed half barrel tank. If needed, you can use a metal clamp, to secure this tubing on so that it doesn't leak from the barbed fitting.

Thread a 12-inch section of twine through the ¼" hole at the top of the half tank. Twist the vinyl tube into a loop so that the other end of the tube end hangs above the sump tank below. Hold it in place by looping the string through the highest point of the tube and tying it in a knot. The highest part of the tube should be approximately 2 inches from the top lip of the half tank and this will be the high water mark of the grow beds. Do the same process to the other half tank.

Using a metal clamp, attach the end of the remaining black vinyl tubing to the outflow of the water pump. Place the pump in the bottom of the Sump tank. Snake the tubing along the outside of the sump tank and grow beds and up the side of the fish tank so that it ends up at the opening of the fish tank. This will return the water from the sump tank back to the fish tank. You can attach the tubing to the fish tank using a metal C clamp.

Using one of the 18-inch lengths of 3-inch diameter PVC, center it on the hole in the grow bed that leads to the bulkhead fitting and the loop siphon. Holding this pipe in place, fill the bed with either of the suggested mediums discussed in this book until it is 1 inch below the rim of the half tank.

Do the same for the second grow bed? Install the heater so that it rests in the fish tank. This can be dangled into the fish tank through the opening on the top. Run two lengths of airline tubing with air stones from the air pump to the fish tank. This will provide the necessary oxygen to your fish. Run two more lengths of airline tubing with air stones from the air pump to the extra water tank that will be used for topping off. This aeration will help dissipate the chlorine from the tap water.

From this point, you begin testing systemic functions, and then cycling. Once everything is all set, you may add your fish and plants. Once plants are added, make sure to turn on the lights and if you wish, set them to a timer to ensure proper amounts of day and night. The lights will be attached to the posts you set up on the four corners of your frame.

An Alternate Option to Media Bed Systems:

Aside from the various ways to create a media bed system, there are numerous ways to get creative with the Nutrient Film Technique also. This may be an option you are considering and many utilize PVC piping to create rows or even levels of grow beds in varying sizes. Depending on your set up, plumbing for these systems would differ greatly and would need to be adapted accordingly. In my opinion, these systems tend to be better suited for herbs and smaller vegetation.

If used for vegetation that will become sizable, the plants will need to be transplanted at a certain point in their growth process. I prefer to maintain a system in which the plants can grow through their entire cycle.

Maintenance

Now that you have the basics down and your Aquaponics garden seems to be running smoothly, you will want to keep it that way so there are general maintenance steps to perform daily, weekly, monthly and seasonally. This chapter will cover these steps as well as advise on how to perform certain maintenance tests. I highly recommend keeping an agenda book where you maintain logs, to do list, supply lists, vendor contacts, and calendar. This will make life so much easier. Staying organized will remove stress factors like remembering what to do and when, allowing you to enjoy the benefits of a healthy, productive garden with an abundance of healthy fish.

Daily

- Feed fish

- Check water

    - Temperature

    - Level

- Check plants

- Growth

- Pests

These are important to check regularly because if the temperatures are off, it can greatly affect your fish including feeding habits. If food is put in the tank and fish don't eat it, it will accumulate and can raise the ammonia levels that are toxic to fish. A proper environment will have healthy fish eating all food within a five-minute time span.

Checking the water levels is also important due to the potential evaporation. Distilled water is pH neutral, so it is the best option to top off the tank. Since everything in an Aquaponics system affects the other, you want to check on your plants too. Make sure there aren't any pests nibbling on your plants and check to see if any plants are ready to be harvested.

Weekly

- Check pH, oxygen, ammonia, nitrite, and nitrate levels.

- Check plumbing for any clogs and make sure everything is running smoothly.

- Prune plants.

Monthly

- Purchase supplies

- Purchase seeds

- Check pump and make sure everything is clear and running as it should be.

Seasonal/ Annual

- Change plants to correspond with the correct season

- Renew any licenses you may need (most expire annually, and each state has its own requirements)

- Work on budget planning for following season/ year

- Determine if you are going to expand or if you need to make more fish purchases

- Make any repairs to Aquaponics area such as greenhouse

- Harvest fish to eat or freeze for a later date

Pest Control

Your garden can be your answer to fresh healthy eating, "farm to table". You grow your garden to feed your family, not to feed pests. Even if your garden is ornamental, that beauty and all that work should not be wasted on pests. Here are some solutions:

- Fight fire with fire. Some bugs are indeed good bugs for your garden.

- Ladybugs eat a long list of the most common garden pests

- Lacewings are also known to eat most common garden pests

- Praying Mantises love to eat and are great bug hunters.

- There are some plants that are insect repellants

- Marigolds: bugs hate the smell and taste (especially mosquitoes and aphids)

- Garlic and chives keep slugs away

- Peppermint is a great ant repellant

- Lavender deters flying and crawling insects and it smells great.

- Of course, you can always go with the traditional bug zappers, sticky strips, and/or a safe bacteria known as BT or Bacillus thuringiensis

Maintenance Tests

It is extremely important to take care of the ecosystem that you have created. If you care for your system, the system will return the favor to you in abundance.

One of the best purchases you can make and ironically one of the less expensive items will be a freshwater master test kit. This kit will have everything included that is necessary to conduct enough tests, throughout the year, for pH, ammonia, nitrites, and nitrates and will take only five minutes of your time. Each kit will advise the proper way to conduct the test and the results desired. This section covers all of the tests that you will need to conduct and how to conduct them.

pH

Changes can happen very quickly in the system and therefore testing the pH balance is important each month. If the pH test demonstrates that the water is not neutral, meaning it is higher in either acid or alkaline, you will need to create balance again. In order to reduce the alkalinity levels because they are registering over 7.0 (neutral), you would need to add some acid to the water until the levels go down to neutral readings.

The suggested acid additive would be hydrochloric acid which can be easily purchased at any home and garden improvement store. Instead of adding the HCL directly to the water in the fish tank, it is advised that you add it to grow beds so that they can do their necessary biofiltration process which will be much safer for your fish. It is also important to remember not to use products specifically made for Aquariums because of their tendency to have high levels of sodium which could be highly detrimental to your plants. The opposite can also occur and you may find that you need to increase your pH levels (lower than 7.0 neutral reading) because there is too much acid present in the fish tank water.

Bicarbonate or Hydroxide compounds of potassium and calcium will aid in increasing your bases and reducing the acid readings. While they neutralize your levels, they work to improve the health of your plants because they are necessary nutrients for your garden. Again, the compound you choose should be administered through the grow beds and not directly into the fish tank water.

Dissolved Oxygen

As discussed earlier, there are definite signs that there is an issue with the oxygen levels in your fish tank water. Your fish may not speak with words, but they can tell you volumes if you pay attention to them and one clear sign that there is an oxygen deficiency is when the fish seem to be gasping for air and spending most of their time at the top of the water. Either way, if the fish are acting funky, something is wrong in the water so you will need to run tests.

If it is the oxygen versus one of the other levels being out of whack, simply run an air pump to increase air flow. Additionally, your plant to fish ratios may need to be adjusted by increasing your grow beds. A popular and efficient kit for testing the dissolved oxygen levels is made by Salifert.

You will also need to monitor your temperature, humidity, light and the water levels, as these can impact the readings of other things you are testing for.

Ammonia, Nitrite, and Nitrate

As discussed earlier, vital to the health of your plants and fish, maintaining a proper Nitrogen Cycle is so important.

The same kit that advised to purchase for pH testing, will give you enough tests to conduct throughout the course of a year for each of these categories as well. If you find that the levels are not at zero which would be evident in a full cycle, then you will need to add minimal amounts of ammonia until the cycle completes and your readings reflect zero ammonia, zero nitrites, and either have nitrate or are in full cycle again reading nitrate at zero.

Conclusion

Thank you for making it through to the end.

For a booming aquaponics system, it's necessary to decide on the proper fish. However it's additionally essential to determine a maintenance routine, particularly for an outside setup. certify to frequently check the water for pH scale, ammonia level, and temperature. Regular testing can help you to notice variations that might be potentially dangerous before they damage your fish or plants. Oftentimes, the process of removing some water and adding water will ensure that balance is maintained. cleansing on a regular basis can help to stop protoctist overgrowth.

Finally, if you found this book useful in any way, a review on Amazon is always appreciated!

WHAT OTHERS ARE SAYING

Strong Enough provides the strength, hope and guidance that families desperately need to nurse their loved ones back to recovery. In these pages we hear the voices of family members who have valiantly prevailed over not only the nightmare of an eating disorder, but over a health system that urgently needs to change.

Associate Professor Warren Ward
Co-author, with Lexi Crouch, of *Renourish: A complete and compassionate guide to recovery from eating disorders*

Strong Enough is a powerful and deeply compassionate contribution to the eating disorders field. By centring the voices of carers, this book brings into sharp focus the realities of supporting a loved one with an eating disorder; experiences that are too often unseen, underestimated, or misunderstood.

The book is also an important reminder that effective eating disorder care does not occur in isolation. The lived experiences shared here underscore the central role of families and carers as essential partners in treatment and recovery. These narratives deepen our understanding of the systemic, relational, and emotional dimensions of eating disorders, and challenge us to reflect on how services, language, and clinical approaches can more effectively support those living with an eating disorder as well as their families and carers.

Jade Gooding
CEO, Australia and New Zealand
Academy for Eating Disorders (ANZAED)

Strong Enough is a quiet companion for parents, siblings and loved ones – honest, vulnerable and deeply reassuring in moments when isolation feels overwhelming.

For anyone supporting a loved one through an eating disorder, this book offers solidarity more than solutions, and sometimes that is exactly what's needed to keep going.

Hugh van Cuylenburg
Mental Health Leader, Founder, The Resilience Project,
best-selling author, co-host The Imperfects Podcast

Strong Enough brings together deeply human accounts from families navigating the reality of supporting someone experiencing an eating disorder, balancing practical guidance with honest stories of grief, fear, and endurance. These stories offer insight into how eating disorders, particularly anorexia and ARFID, can take hold, often quietly and quickly, and profoundly affect the person, their families, and their support networks. Importantly, they also speak to what helps including how understanding, care, and persistence can interrupt the illness and support recovery.

The depth and complexity of these experiences sit alongside clear messages about the value of knowledge, evidence-based care, and working in a collaborative and coordinated way with the person, their family, and the care team. Treatment is an inherently personal experience and must address the whole person, including physical health, mental health, and the broader factors that shape vulnerability and recovery. Whilst risk factors, treatment responses, and recovery pathways may differ, the stories consistently highlight the importance of early support from knowledgeable practitioners, sustained connection, and an aligned approach that tackles the nourishment of the body and mind.

Collectively, the stories are real, valid, and instructive, reminding us that eating disorders affect people and families in different ways and at different points along a broader spectrum of illness and recovery. What unites them is hope: that recovery is possible, that relationships can heal alongside it, and that no one has to face this alone.

I am deeply grateful to the families who have bravely shared their experiences so openly. In connecting with others' stories, families and support people may recognise aspects of their own journey, gain insight into unfamiliar ones, and find reassurance that strength can be built, support is available, and hope can be held even in the most difficult moments.

Dr Sarah Trobe
National Director
National Eating Disorders Collaboration